CHILDREN OF THEIR FATHERS

Children of their Fathers

GROWING UP AMONG
THE NGONI OF NYASALAND

MARGARET READ

LONDON

METHUEN & CO LTD

36 ESSEX STREET · STRAND · WC2

Contents

5

7

CONTENTS

List of Plates

9

Introduction

Like the wooden Ngoni meat dish, this book stands on three firm legs. It is the outcome of lecturing for over twenty years to teachers and students of education from all over the world on how an anthropologist approaches the study of education. It is the result of living for three and a half years in Ngoni villages in Nyasaland, watching how they brought up their children, hearing their reasons for the shaping of that up-bringing, and seeing what use they made of formal education in mission schools. And lastly, since the war ended, young parents in several countries have talked with me now and then about how they were bringing up their children and what they thought of schools in relation to their home training.

I like to think, though it may be self-flattery, that a close study of the home and of parents' attitudes towards the bringing up of their children is an essential complement to the ideas presented to young teachers, and to older ones too for that matter, of what education is and how it works. I am often startled, and driven to furious thinking, when I come across statements like these: 'School is a civilizing place,' from the Harvard Committee on Education in a Free Society; or 'We have to rely on the schools for the training of character' from the Beecher Report on Education in Kenya; or 'The school is an institution specifically established to produce desirable changes in behaviour,' from the opening address to a symposium on Education and Anthropology at Stanford University, California. We all know that there are parents everywhere who are only too thankful to hand over to the schools, or to anyone, the continuous and exacting task of seeing how children behave, watching the development of their individual character and abilities, thinking out and putting into practice ways in which the young barbarians can eventually become useful members of a community. That last word, 'community', is perhaps the clue to those parents, and it seems to me that there are many in western countries and in Africa and India and elsewhere today, who are consciously, and with increasing interest, taking on their shoulders the job of bringing up their children and hoping for co-operation from the school and teachers in that task.

What are these families, the interested ones, aiming at in bringing up their children and what means do they use to forward those aims? Are they chiefly concerned with the way their children fit into and regard the intimate family group of which they are a part, and the larger circle of kinsfolk and relations, sometimes real to children if they live near and meet often, sometimes shadowy if they are seldom seen, sometimes a joy and sometimes a menace to the more intimate family life? Do parents also want their children to fit into the local 'community' whatever it may be, a village, a suburb, a city street? Or are the parents themselves rather conscious of belonging to a selected group of neighbours and friends, and do they want their children, as they grow up, to be identified with this, or a similar group? Do these parents want their children to identify themselves solely or mainly with their own age group in school and in the neighbourhood? Or do they envisage that growing children, even at their most individualistic and aggressive stages, should learn to fit in with younger children, with adults in general and with older people, and should develop attitudes and behaviour which have a wider social significance than those displayed in the classroom and the playground?

These are the kind of questions which many young parents are asking themselves today. Sometimes they get together and talk about the peculiar ideas of teachers about children in general and their children in particular. They wonder how far school standards of behaviour and school codes of morals harmonize or clash with family ideas on behaviour and family ways of living. There is sometimes an attitude of aggressive criticism on both sides, parents and teachers; occasionally it becomes an attitude of cheerful and friendly co-operation; quite often parents and teachers shrug their shoulders with resignation at the gulf which separates home and school, and look for another scapegoat, like an education authority, on which to put the blame.

This situation, which embraces the outlook of parents on their children's present and future, and their attitude towards schools, teachers and education systems in general, is world wide—it knows no national frontiers. When parents and teachers from different countries get down to talking about these questions, they can understand each other's problems in general terms, though they have to explain to each other the specific cultural forms in which these problems appear in each country, with regard to learning and using more than one language for example. In the groups of students to whom I lectured, many of the teachers from overseas were also parents, but very few of them had ever considered the education of their own children in school in relation to the pattern of family and home training in their own society. Many of them discovered an alarming number of problems which demanded their attention—alarming because they were obliged to consider and formulate their own family attitudes towards child training, and at the same time to contemplate and criticize the school education which they had accepted so whole-heartedly as the vital step towards progress for their children and their nation. Every now and then my confidence in the usefulness of this anthropological approach to education was fostered by an angry young man who came up after a lecture and said 'Why was I not told about these things when I was training as a teacher? How can my country begin to understand these things?' From Somaliland and the Sudan, from British Guiana and Jamaica, from Malaya, India and Pakistan, and from all parts of Africa came these indignant reactions, and from those countries and many others I have had in letters over many years references to 'those Ngoni people you used to talk about'.

So it is with young parents and young teachers chiefly in mind, though I hope with some young anthropologists too, that this book has been written. I have for instance avoided as far as possible technical jargon, that seemingly essential language in which anthropologists, educationists and many others wrap up and conceal their hidden mysteries from the common man. In the appendix will be found certain definitions of terms which have crept in and whose use has been inevitable in the Ngoni cultural setting, and also some of the vernacular terms for which I have substituted the nearest English equivalent. Here and there I have had to introduce a vernacular term but there are not many. The book is so arranged that the five narrative chapters (III to VII) follow consecutively. Chapters II and VIII are concerned with an analysis of some of the problems presented by the study, and can be skipped by those who do not like problems but want a straight story. Chapter I is I think essential to a full understanding of the narrative chapters, because Ngoni children were not brought up in a vacuum, but in a very specific political and social situation—as indeed all children are.

There will be plenty of criticism about the material and the focus in this book. Indignant young women will say 'What a poor deal the Ngoni mother had! Did the father and the grandmother really have it all their own way?' The answer is partly that a writer has to use bold outline strokes in painting his picture or it becomes hazy and lacking in purpose; and partly that young Ngoni mothers knew that one day they would be grandmothers and then they would get their own back. Psychologists will say 'But this is all too positive! Positive aims in training, positive methods and, apparently, positive results. Were there no failures and breakdowns in the systems, no cleavages in the society, no maladjusted individuals?' Of course there were. Again the bold outlines have been essential in portraying a situation unfamiliar to many readers. And the rest of the answer to that criticism, as I hinted more than once in the book, lies in studies of individual Ngoni people and how they came out of the training process; and also in studies of the relation of schools and the education given in them to that somewhat rigid and self-consciously controlled Ngoni society. Both of these I hope to write one day, but this book is long enough already.

Young parents the world over are often surprised, and delighted (though not always), at the individual character shown by each of their children. They look in their children for signs of heredity and for evidence of the success or failure of their training. So did the Ngoni, and yet at the end they always came back to 'It is his own human nature'.

M. R.

1. Chief dressed for war-dance

2. Chief dressed for war-dance with wives

3. Chief and his elders in kraal

I

Ngoniland and the People
who lived in it

The homeland

The little country of Nyasaland in Central Africa received
its name from the lake by which Livingstone and those who
followed him penetrated into the interior and reached the
lands and people living round the lake. On the west side
there is a narrow strip of low-lying coastal land. Then a
series of escarpments begin, and up them roads and paths
wind through steep wooded valleys, until the final scarp
leads to the grasslands of the high plateau. Here on the high
plateau the Ngoni settled about the middle of the nineteenth
century, after nearly forty years of trekking from Natal to
Tanganyika. They turned south again at the shores of Lake
Victoria and returned to this land which they had passed
through on their northward march. This high plateau has
great diversity of scenery, and much of it reminded the Ngoni
of the hills and valleys and grasslands of Natal. There are
high mountains with sharp peaks and massive granite
shoulders. Between the ranges of lower grass-covered hills
are shallow valleys where the rain washes down good soil to
the valley bottoms. Sweeps of grassland, bare of trees,
alternate with river valleys where there is a continuous flow
of water, fed by springs and mountain streams.

In the dry season, from April to November, the trees lose
their leaves and the grass gradually dries up till the prevail-
ing colours are gold and brown against the black and grey

rocky outcrops. In September, several weeks before the rains begin, the trees burst out into red foliage, making scarlet rings and patches around the mountains and along the valleys, while through the hard-baked earth spring gladioli and orchids. This is the time of the bush fires when grass is burned and men and boys go hunting. The first rain storms bring a transformation. Fresh green grass covers the land, and scarlet leaves turn bright green on bushes and trees, and later marigolds turn the hillsides golden and yellow arums and red-hot pokers appear along the road-sides.

In making this high plateau their home, the Ngoni chose it primarily for the pasture lands for their cattle. They sited their villages on the ridges or the slopes of the hills, where they had a commanding position, with access to water, good land for cultivation in the shallow dips and river valleys, and woodlands where they could cut poles for their houses and cattle kraals.

The traditional Ngoni village was built in a horse shoe formation round a circular cattle kraal. Larger villages had a central kraal with huts round it, and several other kraals each with its horseshoe grouping of huts. A large village, and there were many of over a hundred huts, seemed at first sight to be a sprawling collection of huts and kraals, with a few tall trees about and several red ant-hills. A pattern of hut sites became apparent, however, once the family and kin-ship grouping was known. Behind each hut was one or more circular grain stores built on platforms, large ones for maize and smaller ones for millet or ground-nuts. In the Central Ngoni kingdom, and sometimes in the Northern kingdom, there were tall reed fences round the huts of leading families, enclosing an open space where household work went on, and wood and grass were stored.

There were two focal points in each village, reproduced on a minor scale in the hamlets round each kraal. One was the 'big house'[1] at the head of the kraal, where the leading

woman had her home. The other was the 'gate'[2] of the kraal
at the opposite end of the enclosure to the 'big house'. The
name by which this 'gate' was known applied also to the
space on each side of the gap in the kraal fence through
which the cattle went out and came in—a gap which was
closed at night with heavy poles. Here at the gate the men
of the village sat by day, ate their meals brought to them by
children from their wives' huts, talked, received strangers,
pursued their crafts, and supervised the return of the cattle
in the evenings.

In and around the main huts within the tall reed fences,
the life of a Ngoni household went on. Some of the huts
were rectangular, others round. All had a veranda built up
above the ground-level and shaded by the house roof. The
back parts of the veranda were often enclosed with mats to
make additional storage space. In old Ngoni households the
open space around the hut was kept swept and mudded and
polished like a floor, so that people could sit there in comfort
and cleanliness as well as on the veranda. Near the house
was one or more little reed platforms about five feet above
the ground, where kitchen utensils, gourds and vegetables
were laid to dry, and which were used to sit under as shelter
from the sun in the hot months. Large and small wooden
pounding mortars and poles, clay pots of every size and
shape, mats for sleeping and for drying grain, baskets for
many purposes, wooden food trays and spoons, gourds of
several shapes, formed the traditional household equipment
always to be seen outside and around the hut, as well as
inside.

In each household, within the main hut, there were two
places of particular significance. One was by the two main
door-posts at the entrance. These posts with the hollow for
the fireplace in the centre of the floor divided the hut into
a right-hand and left-hand side—the men's side and the

[1] and [2] A short list of the vernacular terms for some these common
Ngoni place-names is given at end of the book.

women's. For all ceremonies the men sat on the right side, and the women on the left, the place of honour for the leading man and woman being by the main door-posts. No young man or woman ever thought of sitting near them. The other place of significance lay between the fire and the back of the hut on the right-hand side; it was known as the 'place of the spirits', the 'ancestors' corner', where the baskets and spears and other ritual objects were kept which were used in the ancestral cult. Only the owner of the hut or those taking part in the ritual could approach this corner.

In this land, into the cultural pattern of Ngoni village and household life, the Ngoni children were born. In such villages and homes they passed their earlier years, and grew from boys and girls to young adults.

The Ngoni kingdoms

When the Ngoni made parts of Nyasaland their homeland they set up conquest states on the pattern which they had been familiar with in southern Africa. Where they settled, they either conquered the local peoples who lived in that area, or accepted their submission. Until the British administration was established the Ngoni carried on wars and raids against neighbouring peoples to enlarge the boundaries of their kingdoms. As a conquest state, similar to that of the Ndebele in Southern Rhodesia, the population of the Ngoni kingdoms was of mixed origin, some whose ancestors came from Natal, some from the territories passed through on their northward march, and some from Nyasaland itself.

The kingdoms were organized on a centralized pattern with the Paramount Chief as supreme ruler and subordinate chiefs under him. The Ngoni code of law operated in the courts of the chiefs, and, as they proudly said, 'there was one law for all people'. Military service was required from all young men, and each territorial chief had to bring his quota of warriors to the Paramount's village when a war summons went out. Military service, obedience to the law,

recognition of the Paramount's supremacy were therefore
the main traditional forces uniting the mixed populations
in the kingdoms.

Ngoni society

Although all people living in the Ngoni kingdoms were
subjects of the Paramount, only those who could trace their
descent from families who crossed the Zambezi River were
recognized as 'true Ngoni'. Four main characteristics marked
off this true Ngoni group from the rest. The first was their
clan name, giving them an authentic origin south of the
Zambezi. The second was a marriage contract sealed by
handing over cattle, which established the offspring as
'children of their fathers', for, as they said, 'where the
children are, the cattle are not'. The third was patrilineal
descent and inheritance through the male line, and patrilocal residence at marriage, so that the wife came as a
'stranger' to her husband's people and village. The fourth
was membership of a 'house', the social group of male
members of Ngoni families with their wives and children
round a leading woman. Everyone was born into a 'house'
and the men remained in it for life, the women until their
marriage. For special reasons children could be adopted
into another house than the one into which they were born.

In a few of the smaller villages of North Nyasaland, con-
sisting of ten to fifteen huts, all the men were true Ngoni,
descendants of one or more former warriors in the same
regiment, who had chosen to set up their own villages after
the British had taken over the country. In such villages the
cultural pattern of Ngoni life could be seen clearly, but they
were not typical of the Ngoni kingdoms. There was always
a mixture of peoples in the larger villages, dominated by a
group of true Ngoni families.

This group of true Ngoni families were the social and
cultural aristocracy of these villages. They considered themselves superior to and distinct from the other ethnic elements

in the village, whom they regarded as inferior not only because they had been conquered, but because they disliked
and despised their way of living. This sense of separateness
from and of superiority to the non-Ngoni elements in the
villages had its counterpart in the close ties which existed
with Ngoni families in other villages. These ties were reinforced socially by 'dynastic' or inter-clan marriages, and
politically through the hierarchy of courts and officials
leading up to the Paramount's court and entourage.

The Ngoni aristocracy endeavoured to maintain their
traditional ways of living and of bringing up their children
in the face of changes creeping in from the non-Ngoni
elements in the village, as well as from external European
influences. The maintenance of Ngoni ways of living and
cultural patterns of behaviour depended on three main elements in village society. One was the degree of integration
between the Ngoni men in their house groups and in village
society as a whole. This was most evident in chiefs' villages,
and in the villages belonging to the heads of clans. The
second element was the number of wives of true Ngoni
families who had married into the village, thus combining
the influence of husband and wife, or rather of father and
mother, in bringing up children on the Ngoni pattern. The
third element was the number and influence of senior women
of Ngoni families, either wives of older men in the village,
or widows of former leaders. This senior women's group,
many of whom were addressed as 'mother' by the Ngoni
fathers of young families, were a formidable force in maintaining tradition, by advising their sons, coercing their
daughters-in-law, and holding on to their authority at every
stage of the children's development.

Life in two Ngoni villages

I am going briefly to sketch in, as a general background
for the following chapters, the main features of two villages,
in one of which I lived for several months, in the other for

a few weeks. They were both dominated by important Ngoni families, and both the headquarters of subordinate chiefs. They both represented that blend of old and new in Ngoni life which was continually keeping the anthropologist on her toes.

Enkodlweni was far from main roads and centres of modern life. When I first went there my lorry cut a swathe of grass knee-high on the so-called road to the village, and the radiator, choked with grass seed, boiled all the time. I lived in the mud-and-wattle hut maintained by the chief for visiting teachers and missionaries opposite the school, a four-standard school under an able young headmaster, well educated and well trained. He and his schoolboys, the resident evangelist and the court clerk represented the new elements in village life. Yet they were not cut off from the Ngoni way of life—on the contrary they were very much part of it and very proud of being Ngoni. The school had been taught in the Ngoni language, akin to old Zulu, until a few years before my visit, and the children were still given Ngoni proverbs to write in their copy-books. Several of the older people had books in their huts written in Zulu as well as in English, and Ngoni was still spoken as the home language in many of the households. The older women knew the traditional special vocabulary used by women only, and dressed their hair in the high chignon style. Proverbs were quoted often in the court and in church; stories of war against the Bemba people in Northern Rhodesia forty years ago were told by the kraal gate as if they happened last year. Several leading Ngoni clans were represented in the village, and each had their own praise songs and forms of addressing their ancestors.

The old evangelist, himself a member of a famous clan, had been threatened, thirty years before, with death by the former chief if he continued to teach and preach. He stayed, notwithstanding, and had become one of the trusted counsellors of the present chief. During the day he joined the

senior men who related to me historical events, family genea-
logies, war-songs and other Ngoni traditional knowledge,
including the ideas and methods of bringing up Ngoni children. In the evenings the schoolboys gathered by my hut to
practise their English, to discuss their school work and their
plans for the future. The tsetse menace had for some time
been threatening the cattle and losses were considerable.
The boys wanted above all to emigrate and find work so
that they could earn money to send home to their fathers to
buy more cattle, pay taxes, buy clothes, guns and ammuni-
tion, for it was lion country.

Out of the thirty-one households in the village, twenty-
five belonged to the men of Ngoni clans. There were nine
elderly widows of Ngoni leading families, and of the younger
women eighteen were true Ngoni. There was therefore both
among the men and the women, and in the senior and
younger age-groups, a high proportion of those who were
true Ngoni and who practised the Ngoni way of living. It
was a village where Ngoni cultural patterns were very much
in evidence, and where the school and the church, repre-
senting modern developments, were closely integrated with
village life.

Emcakateni was just off a main road and as easily acces-
sible as Enkodlweni was remote. It was perched on a hill-top
in a commanding position, and was much larger, with a
hundred and twenty-two households compared with thirty-
one. There were several kraals and many cattle, no tsetse
menace, but lions in the neighbourhood which more than
once attacked the kraal at night. Outsiders, that is of non-
Ngoni clans, who had money, had married into the chief's
and other leading families, and these households possessed
well-built brick houses. I lived in a grass-and-pole hut inside a fence, near the compound of the big house. There was
no school in the village, and the nearest one was run by a
mission disliked by the leading Ngoni. The boys spent all
their time with the cattle, or hunting or practising crafts.

There were musicians and craftsmen there, as at Enkodl-weni. All the senior Ngoni men knew Ngoni history, used proverbs in the courts and in conversation, and two or three senior men knew and carried out the ritual of the ancestor cult. The new element in this village was due to economic influences rather than missionary and educational. Most of the men had learned to read and write Nyanja while away at work, but no one knew more than a few words of English, and only one or two of the leading men, and no women, spoke Ngoni.

The men of the leading Ngoni families formed a closely knit group for purposes of village affairs, social life and ritual performances. There was a group of senior Ngoni women who exerted a powerful influence in all matters concerned with household life and the bringing up of children. But out of a total of one hundred and twenty-one households, only thirty-seven belonged to men of Ngoni clans, and there were only thirty-two women of Ngoni clans including both the older and the younger groups of women. The aristocratic group here was small in comparison with Enkodl-weni, but the influence of their ways of living was proportionately much stronger. The Ngoni men and women of leading families were very conscious of their cultural distinction and also of their relatively small numbers, and many were the complaints about 'those other people who are spoiling our land'.

Political and social changes

When the British took over the administration of Nyasaland between 1891 and 1901, the Ngoni kingdoms received no special recognition. Their chiefs, called by the administration principal village headmen, and their heads of clans called village headmen, were relegated to the same position *vis-à-vis* the administration as the local peoples. Part of the Central Ngoni kingdom was cut off from the rest by the treaty demarcating the Nyasaland boundary from Portuguese East

Africa. All males had to pay taxes to the government, at first in kind and later in cash, thus hastening the advent of a money economy. Most drastic of all the changes was the ban on warfare, which cut at the roots of Ngoni political organization, and at their system of training their young men.

In the Northern Ngoni kingdom, the Scottish Mission preceded the administration by more than twenty years, and were largely responsible for a peaceful take-over of the area. In the Central kingdom there was a brief war of resistance, in which the Ngoni armies were dispersed and the Paramount killed on his way to trial. In this area mission activity, under several missions, never achieved, especially in education, the ascendancy which the Scottish Mission achieved among the Ngoni in the North.

As one result of the cessation of warfare, and of school education leading to paid employment, there was an economic redistribution of wealth among the Ngoni. Formerly wealth had been associated with political power, and the Paramounts and their subordinate chiefs and heads of clans had command of large herds of cattle, received the spoils from wars and raids, and used the labour of conquered villages to cultivate the land. After the missions and government were established, men with schooling began to earn money as teachers, clerks and mechanics, and so to command financial resources which were not available to the traditional leaders. The young men responded to the labour recruitment which became a permanent feature in Nyasaland from the 1890s, and they went far afield to many types of work.

It was evident, just before World War II, that the Ngoni kingdoms had had a profound shock from which they never fully recovered, in spite of the recognition of their Paramount Chiefs by the Native Authorities Ordinance in 1934. The older men looked back with nostalgia to what they called 'the time of peace, when the Europeans were not here to trouble us'. These older men were known as 'the generation of former days', because they had taken part in warfare as young men, and had known the independence and supremacy of the Ngoni kingdoms. The expression 'everything is finished now' was often on their lips, especially when faced by new demands from the government, or by rebellious attitudes from their former subject peoples.

'The middle generation' was the term applied to the men who had as children known the Ngoni kingdoms in their prime. Though they had never fought as warriors nor been enrolled in an age-regiment, some of them had gone to the wars as young boys, carrying the gear for their older brothers. Many of these men, especially in the North, came under the influence of the missions, and became teachers, clerks, ministers and hospital assistants, married Christian wives and brought up their children in Christian, but Ngoni Christian, families. These men never lost their attachment to the Ngoni way of living, and many of them had made a successful synthesis of the old and the new ways. They stood, as they said, 'between' the generations, for they knew and understood both sides of an immensely different way of living and standard of values. Their children were 'the generation of today', who had no personal experience of past Ngoni ascendancy, and who took mission schooling and working for wages as a normal feature of their life.

When I lived in Ngoni villages, such as those described briefly in this chapter, Ngoni values and attitudes dominated social relationships. There was a determined struggle on the part of all responsible for child training to inculcate these Ngoni ideas and ways of living. The senior men and women were aware of the constant and increasing infiltration into their way of living of ideas, attitudes and behaviour coming from other ethnic groups in their midst. In addition their culture was being undermined by European influences in the schools, in the money economy, and from modern political developments, emphasizing an all-Nyasaland sentiment rather than loyalties based on ethnic grouping. Ngoni pride of race, and a consciousness that they had a culture worth preserving, inspired them to put up a fight against all that threatened the values inherent in their way of living. It was perhaps the struggle of a disappearing aristocracy. But Ngoni fathers thought that the principles of education on which they brought up their children were worth a struggle.

II

Growing up among the Ngoni

The approach to this study

Among the several titles used to describe this and similar kinds of studies, such as child development, child study, child training, socialization, I think the ugly but useful term socialization most nearly covers the theme of this particular study. I much prefer, mainly on aesthetic grounds, the non-technical, non-committal expression 'growing-up', used in the title of this chapter and established long ago in the pioneer study of Margaret Mead in New Guinea. I realize, however, that this title could be misleading if readers expected a psychological as well as an anthropological approach, and looked for psychological analyses and techniques applied to children at different stages of their development. The arguments for a joint approach by anthropologists and psychologists are well known, and have been clearly stated in the introduction to Dr H. M. Ammar's recent book: *Growing up in an Egyptian Village*. On the whole, in most studies of 'growing up', the psychological emphasis is much stronger. We frequently find descriptions of infancy and the early years of childhood set out in psychological terms familiar to western society, without what I consider as the essential complement, an equal emphasis on the aims and methods of that particular society in training its children. This complementary study could and should be predominantly the task of the social anthropologist, but it is one which has hitherto not attracted a great deal of attention from anthropologists in their field studies.

One more word about 'growing up'. It has in popular language often been associated with 'he just growed, like Topsy', implying a minimal amount of direction and a maximum amount of free response by a child to all external stimuli. No one can, of course, control a child's inner response to direction and training, but more often than not a child can and does learn, for a variety of reasons, to show the overt response expected by the adults who are bringing him up. The potential conflict in a child between his inner and overt responses lies within the field of individual psychological studies, and I am well aware that in this respect as in others this study is incomplete.

However, as I endeavoured to suggest in the introduction, this is a society-directed study in which the focus is on how adults bring up their children to fit into their society and to perpetuate their cultural values. The emphasis, therefore, here is on the training of children as part of the social life and cultural aims of the community, and the children's response is regarded from the angle of how they learn what the adults have to teach. Here and there I think I may have lost the thread of learning in following the thread of teaching—too close a concentration on two foci can produce a squint which is not always the best way of looking at situations. The main emphases in the training of Ngoni children, perhaps of children everywhere, are on behaviour, on skills and on knowledge. If we want to understand the process carried out by adults in training their children in any of these respects, we have to keep asking the questions, familiar to educationalists: what is taught? Who teaches it? When do they do it? In what contexts do they do it? It would be tedious in the extreme to keep on asking these questions in the following chapters, and to use this method would certainly break or hopelessly entangle the threads of learning and teaching in Ngoni society. Those questions however have been in the background and implicit all through the narrative chapters from III to VII. If readers cannot find answers to them somewhere, then there have been some vital omissions in the narrative.

Clues to this study

In relating this study to other field studies and analyses of socialization techniques and processes, I have not attempted to present here any general assessment of similar or related studies, much less any review of the field as a whole, since I have touched on both in earlier publications.[1] Instead I have brought into this chapter one or two clues or guide lines from other sources which seemed to me to elucidate some of my problems, particularly in regard to four main aspects of this study, which have already been mentioned in Chapter I and which to a large extent set the limits and determine the emphases of this book. The 'true Ngoni' were a society within a society, a distinct cultural group within the Ngoni kingdom. This society of theirs had sharp edges, definable and recognizable limits, and that partly accounted for their own awareness of themselves as distinct from, though at so many points connected with, the neighbouring peoples. Their culture, that is their way of living within this society, had definite values which they strove to maintain, and this was one of the reasons why the ideal Ngoni personality pattern, and their endeavour to see it reproduced in each child, was easy to recognize. In order to safeguard their society and maintain their culture they exercised a fairly rigid social control over the upbringing of their children, which resulted in something approaching a 'system' of training and educating children. Set against this conservation of traditional values however was the reality and extent of changes due to external circumstances mentioned at the end of Chapter I. In the face of these changes the Ngoni showed that they could adapt some of them to their own purposes, and they made use of the schools, for example, once they approved of them, to help adjust their

[1] See Appendix (i)

31

society and particularly their children to new ways of living and thinking. These then are the four aspects of the study for which I sought clues: awareness of their society, definite cultural values, social control of bringing up children, adaptation to external change.

In alluding to the following authors and the ways in which they furnished clues for this study, I hope it may lead readers to consult the full works for themselves, and indeed to explore others which can be found in any good bibliography on socialization or on personality and culture. Over many years I have read and re-read Ralph Linton's *The Cultural Background of Personality*, in order to throw light on my own studies and to illustrate my lectures. When assembling the material for this Ngoni study I welcomed and followed up his thesis that 'some groups are much more conscious of the existence of culture and much more prone to generalize about behaviour than others'. That and other passages certainly helped to throw light on the Ngoni awareness of their own culture and their articulateness about behavioural training.

Linton also assisted me, though I did not completely agree with all his analysis, in placing cultural values in their relation to the accepted personality patterns. I used here other clues, and notably those provided by Monica Wilson in her book *Good Company* and John Whiting in his field manual for studies of child training. The Nyakusa values, brought out so clearly by Professor Wilson, I was able to compare with Ngoni values. Among the Nyakusa, 'good company', dignity, display, decency, wisdom, were constantly stressed and behaviour on these lines was commended by adults. The Nyakusa were a homogeneous and secure people, whose system of age-villages was unique among the surrounding peoples and a powerful force in maintaining and developing socially desirable forms of behaviour. Dr Whiting, in his field study manual, suggests eight 'systems of behaviour' for field workers to observe and classify in terms of individual

4. Chief waiting to hear cases

5. Chief with his elders in his court-house

6, 7.
Pounding maize

child behaviour. Five of them appear to suggest values some of which have a place either in Nyakusa or Ngoni ideal personality patterns: self-reliance, obedience, responsibility, sociability, dominance. But there is at least one major difference between the approaches of Professor Wilson and Dr Whiting to the training of children. Professor Wilson is describing the values of Nyakusa adults and their effect on the bringing up of children. Dr Whiting has selected from a series of cultures certain typical or common forms of behaviour which might be displayed by children. These forms of behaviour might represent general social values, but they are not set in the context of any one culture, and the criterion is whether an observer saw a child displaying sociability rather than whether the society desired their children to show sociability and took steps to encourage it. This book was after all a manual to be usable in a number of cultural situations. His emphasis is nevertheless on the observed behaviour of selected children, and illustrates my point made in the early pages of this chapter; whereas Professor Wilson's emphasis was on the adult ideal personality to which, it was hoped, Nyakusa children would conform.

The existence of a 'system' in the upbringing of children, a system set up by a society and under its control, posed a number of questions. Clyde Kluckhohn in several of his books has for a long time provided me with clues in the study of 'systems', and many of these clues are summarized in the chapter on Personality and Culture in his book *Mirror for Man*. Especially in two directions these clues have proved helpful: in his distinction between two kinds of cultural learning, technical and regulatory, or acquiring skills and learning to behave, the latter taking place in the early years of chilhhood, and acquiring skills in later years; and in his theme of predictability, illustrated in this quotation: 'A definition of socialization in any culture is the predictability of an individual's daily behaviour in various defined situations. . . . When a person behaves most of the time as others do in following cultural routines, he is then socialized.'

I have deliberately carried on the study of the Ngoni 'system' through what are generally called the adolescent years. In so doing I followed some of the clues in Professor Linton's discussion of how different societies treated adolescence and its alleged problems. Dr H. M. Ammar also provided a clue in his account of the sharp gulf in the Egyptian village of Silwa between child and adult, between the ways of childhood and the values of adulthood. But in sorting out the problems which the Ngoni study presented, I have drawn also on my recollection of discussions with Dr Kurt Hahn at Gordonstoun about the place of adolescents in society, and whether what is commonly called 'an awkward age' is necessarily part of a child's growing up. Two particular contributions of Kurt Hahn's have thrown light on the young Ngoni adult. One was the correlation between physical stages of growth and social responsibility; and the other was the close connexion between acquiring skills which are socially valuable and essential, and the general maturing of the young adult, especially in his growing confidence in himself and in his self-respect.

On the fourth point, the effect of external changes such as schools on child training, I found much that was useful in Oscar Lewis' *Life in a Mexican Village*. It seems to me he has gone further than most anthropologists in examining the school and its methods and ideas in relation to a traditional culture and society. From an educational as well as from an anthropological angle, H. M. Ammar's analysis of the place of schools in Egyptian villages is also very stimulating.

Social horizons of Ngoni children

Most studies of child training concentrate, or at least place the main emphasis, on a child in his family setting, with the connotation of a family in the western individual sense of father, mother and their children. The subsequent chapters

34

of this book, especially Chapters IV and V will show how
the organization of Ngoni society and the cultural way of
living in it, necessarily surrounded the life of children and
the training given to them with a much wider horizon. We
shall talk about the family, the household, the village as the
setting of Ngoni child life, but these terms have to be in-
terpreted according to the Ngoni social organization,
sketched very briefly in Chapter I and set out at length in my
earlier book *The Ngoni of Nyasaland*. Looked at from another
angle, we can see that a young child's horizon in Ngoni
villages was limited at first to what he saw around him and
the people who had daily or frequent contact with him and
who understood and supplied his daily needs. But that circle
of people forming a young child's contacts was from the
beginning much wider than the individual family which a
child was born into. When he began to run about and to
pass beyond the restricted confines of the household, it was
as we shall see, the duty and responsibility of all Ngoni
adults to notice his behaviour and correct him when necessary.

The relationships inside the large Ngoni families, between
one family and another in a Ngoni village, with related
families in other villages, with all members of the same clan
living in an area—these were threads in the web of kinship
and clanship which united the Ngoni people. These threads
were also inseparable from the political links between the
people and their territorial chief, and between the whole
people and the Paramount, the head of the kingdom. The
difference, however, between the Ngoni kingdom under the
Paramount which included all his subjects of Ngoni and non-
Ngoni ethnic groups, and the Ngoni aristocracy in the
villages was a profound difference. It was the latter who
understood, appreciated and sought to hand on to their
children Ngoni ways of living based on Ngoni values. Hence
in most villages there were sharp distinctions between standards of behaviour within Ngoni families and in non-Ngoni

families. It was, however, demanded from Ngoni children
that they should behave in the socially approved manner to
everyone, and not only to their Ngoni kin and fellow clans-
men. And it was evident in non-Ngoni families that there was
often some attempt to teach Ngoni standards of behaviour
to their children, but that such attempts broke down when
their family system was not organized to enforce the necessary training.

The goals of Ngoni child training

Ngoni adults, and especially the senior men and women who
were in control of the training of children and themselves
deeply conscious of the traditional values of their society,
summed up the aims of the upbringing of children in one
word 'respect'. The vernacular term *ulemu*—in the old
Ngoni language *hlonipa*—is a concept very difficult to trans-
late adequately, certainly to convey its full meaning in a
single English word or phrase. The nearest terms are honour
and respect, and though in some contexts it is often translated as politeness, that is too limited a term. In fact they
had another vernacular term to express courtesy which was
to them one way of showing respect. The concept of *ulemu*
included the recognition that a particular person or office
was entitled to honour; that all behaviour to that person
must express respect; and that by showing respect in language, posture and action, a child or adult so behaving, shared
in that honour which they were acknowledging. Conversely,
through failing to convey respect, a person, whether child
or adult, was 'ashamed' and lost face accordingly. I have
just said that a particular person was entitled to honour and
therefore to respect in the behaviour of others. The Ngoni
said that was the origin of the concept, and it was demonstrated in the punctilious observance of etiquette to all
chiefs, and to all leading men and women by everyone else.
But there was an extension of this concept to include all
older people, and Ngoni children were expected to show

respect to all adults, whether Ngoni or not, whether of their family, or helpers in the household, or former captives. If children did not so behave to old and poor people, they were punished and made to feel ashamed as if they had failed to honour their own relatives.

A Ngoni elder when speaking of the testimony of early travellers in Ngoniland to the good manners found in Ngoni households said: 'Such honouring of each other came to the Ngoni because they liked living together without any scattering as was the custom of other Nyasaland people. . . . . Such honour was not shown by young people for fear of being beaten, but because all children were well taught that this behaviour was right and proper for the upbuilding of the land.'

The emphasis in this quotation is clearly on the connexion between personal behaviour and the integrity and prosperity of the Ngoni kingdom. When Ngoni elders were talking about child training and its effect on the future of the Ngoni people, they made constant reference to 'those who spoil the land'. The phrase was the same as taking the roof off a hut, i.e. destroying it for the purpose for which it was built. This determined emphasis on behaviour illustrated the Ngoni intention of regulating personal contacts within their society, so that harmonious relations would build up the society which quarrels and factions would destroy, and indeed had partly destroyed in some of the historic secessions from the kingdom. Harmonious personal relations are perhaps the covert if not the overt aim of all human societies from the individual family outwards. We see this however in sharp outline in Ngoni life, partly because they were acutely aware of the vulnerability from external influences of their society and way of living.

Two very ancient folk-tales illustrate Ngoni thinking about keeping their kingdom and society intact and maintaining their code of polite behaviour.

The first was taken down by me from a very old man who

37

had heard it from his grandmother. She had been a young Ngoni woman at the time the Ngoni crossed the Zambezi, and hence this story was said to have had its origin in the Ngoni former homeland in Natal.

The story of Heva

At the beginning of the creation of the world there was a woman of reddish colour whose name was Golela, and she had two children. The name of the older one was Heva, and of the second one Malusi. My grandmother, Madakacha, said that Malusi was the cause of our herds of cattle becoming smaller. When Malusi was herding cattle on the river plains where they were feeding, he kept on disturbing them and driving some away from the rest.

At this time Heva was staying with his mother. Her work was to keep watch over the sun so that the birds did not peck it, and Heva helped her by flapping away the flies which were troubling her.

Their mother Golela asked Heva, 'Where is your brother? What is he doing?' Heva replied, 'There he is yonder, disturbing your cattle on the river plain.' Then Golela called Malusi and said to him, 'Go. Choose what you want and depart. Go with them far away. What is left here is for Heva.'

After Malusi went away, all that remained on the river plain belonged to Heva, including the animals and the birds and the crops, but the cattle were reduced in number.

My grandmother used to say about this story, 'We who are descended from Heva are the victims of this separation between the brothers. Because Malusi in the beginning of the world took away many of the cattle of his mother's house, we have never had large herds of cattle since then.'

The Ngoni saw in the archaic form of this folk-tale several meanings. It was one of their traditional creation myths. It supported their belief that they were once owners of vast herds of cattle. It emphasized the relationships between brothers in their mothers' 'house', and the vesting of the rights over cattle in the male members of the house. But the chief reason why it was told to the children was as a warning against quarrels between brothers, which led to their separating from each other and dividing the property of a house instead of keeping it intact.

The second folk-tale was always known as the story of Brass-Rod, the translation of the name of the elder sister.

The story of Brass-Rod

A certain chief had two daughters. The name of the older one was Ntonga-ye-Tusi, and the younger one was Mbikazi. Ntonga-ye-Tusi, because she was the daughter of a chief, wanted to go and seek in marriage a chief who had a country of his own. So she set out on her travels, leaving her younger sister at home. When she met crippled people on the road, she was polite to all of them, and helped them and made them comfortable.

When she arrived at a certain place she went to the men of the village and they asked her, 'What have you come here for?' She replied, 'I want to seek a chief in marriage.' The man said, 'Well, our chief is a snake, but don't be afraid. When he visits you in the hut he will come with a whistling wind.'

They made her enter a hut and she stayed there quietly saying nothing, while they prepared for the wedding. Suddenly she heard the wind and knew it was the coming of the chief. The chief asked the elders of the village 'Whose wedding are you preparing for?' They said, 'It is for your wedding O Chief and yonder is your bride.' Ntonga-ye-Tusi stayed silent in her hut. She 'sewed up her heart' and was brave. Suddenly the snake-chief entered the hut and coiled round her body and put his head on her heart, saying to himself, 'Let me listen. Perhaps she is afraid.' But she was not afraid.

So they took each other in marriage. The people told her, 'Now then, give him watery gruel for his food and put it for him in the fire hole.' When the gruel was poured out there, he sucked it up because he had no teeth.

Some time after this Ntonga-ye-Tusi rose up to go and see the people at her home. When she got there her younger sister saw her fine clothes and was jealous of her. She said to herself, 'I too am going to the place where my big sister went to get married.'

So Mbikazi rose up and went on her travels. But she treated badly all the crippled people she met, and did not pity those who were carrying heavy loads, and used insulting language to many. When she arrived at the village of the chief who was a snake, the people received her politely and made her go into a hut for the wedding. They told her, as they had told her sister, that she should 'sew up her panic' and not be afraid because the chief was a big snake who came with a wind. When the chief came Mbikazi did not receive him quietly as her sister had done. She ran to and fro in the hut and cried out 'Alas! Alas! What have I found?' Then she trod on the tail of the snake-chief and he was angry and said, 'In what manner have you come? Have you come with insults to call me names and to tread on me?' He caught her and beat her so hard that the village elders begged him to spare her. So he left her in the hut.

When Mbikazi cooked gruel for the chief, she was careless and left a lump in it. The chief sucked his gruel but the lump stuck in his throat and choked him. He wriggled and fainted. The girl ran away, but the people of the village gathered round him, lamenting. Then the small lump came out and the chief recovered, and said, 'Where has she gone?'

He went after her until he reached her home and there he coiled up near the well. When the women went to draw water, they threw down their pots and ran away, and reported that there was a wild beast at the well. Ntonga-ye-Tusi wondered if it could be her husband, so she went to the well and sat near her husband, and they touched hands and saluted each other.

At first the village people ridiculed Ntonga-ye-Tusi because she had played such a trick on them and had gone off and married a wild beast. But she paid no attention and took her husband into her hut.

Then the village people said to her, 'We want to make your husband all right, so that he may stand upright. Don't be afraid and don't weep'—for she was already weeping, fearing that they might harm her husband.

They made the chief go into another hut and they shut the door and set fire to the hut and burned it. His bones burst asunder, and they picked them up and put them in a pit with a gourd full of oil and some iron rattles. Then they sat beside the pit. Suddenly they heard the rattles ringing far down inside and they hurried to take off the stone covering the pit. They saw coming out of the pit a good-looking man of a very handsome red appearance, wearing a head-ring.[1] They acclaimed him and said, 'Here indeed is our son-in-law.' This chief was courteous and well clad. He became the husband of Ntonga-ye-Tusi, later he married Mbikazi also.

This story had many allusions to Ngoni culture past and present. The emphasis on 'red colour' here, as in the story of Heva, recalled the Ngoni belief that they were originally a red, not a black, people. In old days, chiefs' daughters sometimes chose their own husbands, so Brass-Rod and her sister were following an old custom. When the snake-chief, after his transformation, married the younger sister, it was as a subsidiary wife, called by the special title of *nhlanzi*. Such a marriage to a sister of the first wife was regarded as a compliment to the parents of the girl and a recognition of of their careful training of the first wife.

[1] The head-ring was the distinguising mark of the warrior who had served in the army and was allowed to marry.

The moral, which was always repeated at the end as part of the story, was that children were warned not to show unkindness to people but to treat them well so that people would bless them. They were reminded that the older sister showed the qualities of pity, courage and obedience, while the younger sister did not hesitate to display disgust and fear and carelessness. It was the older sister who had her ultimate reward as leading wife of a handsome chief, while the younger sister, as a subsidiary wife, had to take second place.

These two folk-tales were popular among the children, even though they were so different from the animal folk-tales, full of humour and absurdities. The children used to shiver with excitement over the Brass-Rod story, especially the little girls, and the boys sucked in their breath when the wind blew and snapped their fingers for the rattling in the pit. Because the stories were serious and had a didactic purpose, Ngoni fathers approved of them, and encouraged the grandmothers to tell them often in order that the children might remember the moral.

Learning how to behave

Ngoni villages, like the whole Ngoni kingdom, had an efficient system of communication between individuals and groups, but whereas the kingdom had a network of official messengers continually moving between the capital and the outlying sections, the village 'intercom' depended on the children. At any time of day, from first light till after dark, children were moving about the village from one hut to another, from a hut to the kraal gate, taking messages, summoning people, carrying food, reporting arrivals. The messages and summons were all at the bidding of the adults. When a child was called to take a message, he had to respond immediately wherever he was, and run to hear what he was wanted for. Someone calling a child's name, followed by a long drawn out 'Yo—o—o', punctuated all the hours of daylight in a village. When a child was told to call someone older, on reaching them he had to bend one knee, or sit down, and say in a low but clear voice: 'They are calling you.' If a child was sent to call another child to his father because he had a scolding to administer, the bad child had to listen with head bent down, not saying a word or making a sound until the father had finished all he had to say, whether the accusation was just or not. If the child forgot himself and answered back or made excuses, the onlookers would beat the child for being rude to his father. If when taking a message a child had to pass a line or a group of people, he had always to go in front of them, never behind, bending forward from the waist and murmuring as he went by, 'I am before your eyes.' If a child had to give an adult a food basket or any other object, he had to offer it with both hands and bend slightly over it; and when he received it back he always did so with both hands outstretched and bent head.

Acting as messengers constantly, and no child was immune from being called if he or she was in the village, impressed on children from their early years the chief behavioural skills of language and deportment. Taking a message was always a formal occasion, and standards of behaviour in language, posture and gesture were rigidly enforced. We shall see in later chapters how very small children were first taught to thank people for gifts or in response to a greeting, and later to greet people politely themselves. The correct terms in which to address or to refer to relatives formed another stage in learning language skills, and later on came reminders about the use of pronouns and the use of the second person singular and plural of verbs, the first to equals only, the second to all adults, with the third person plural for chiefs and 'great ones'. About the age of five or six a child was told: 'When your mother speaks to a stranger she says "Please (you) sit here". You should speak like this to all people you must honour. Only rude people speak that other way—people who do not know how to thank and how to honour, not like the Ngoni who know these things.'

Correction of bad behaviour, even if thoughtless or careless, was just as often carried out by older children as by
adults. I used to hold a 'children's hour' now and then round
the fire in my compound, or a honey party if I had been
given some wild honey. These occasions were open to all and
were enthusiastically organized by the older children of leading Ngoni families. They pushed the children into some sort
of order, whether sitting or standing, or marching round the
honey-pot to stick one finger in and lick it as they passed.
When we were sitting round the fire there was always due
regard for family ranking, the places immediately on my
right and left being the places of honour. Children of non-
Ngoni families were sharply rebuked if they failed to respond
to my greeting or say farewell, and shyness was never admitted as an excuse. Scathing remarks were dealt out to any who
did not say the correct formal thanks for the honey. 'You,
fellow-villager, you are with the Ngoni now. Say "thank you"
to the lady or she will think you are a wild animal from the
bush, unable to speak.' Bad behaviour was not only corrected
by adults with beating and rebukes. Sometimes the more
indirect form of a proverb was used, especially to correct unkindness, lack of generosity, boasting or bragging. When
someone said with biting emphasis: 'Strength breaks the
handle,' it was enough to deflate a young (or an old) brag-
gart. When children plagued their elders to give them something, they rounded on the children with: 'Give! Give! that
is to snatch. The child of a free man only gives.' This was
invariably effective with Ngoni children who hung their
heads in shame at the very idea of being thought the child of
a captive. Proverbs, except ones like those quoted which
were very often used, were generally enigmatic, and the
meaning was hidden rather than obvious. In a mixed gather-
ing of children and adults, a proverb might suddenly be
dropped like a stone into a pond. The conversation rippled
away into silence, and the boy or girl who had refused to
share some peanuts or had been boasting began to wonder

to himself: 'Can that be for me? No? Yes? It *is* me. I am ashamed.' No one said anything but the shamed one took the first chance of slipping away to avoid further public notice. The use of proverbs in this way were an effective way of making a child learn for himself and apply the lesson; and with children, as with adults, the use of proverbs was a way of 'saving face' when a direct rebuke in the presence of others would have caused overwhelming shame.

Ngoni ideas about nature and nurture

This fixed code of social behaviour between persons was instilled by Ngoni adults into their children from their early years. By the time they had their second teeth, a significant stage to the Ngoni, they were expected to conduct themselves towards other people according to this code. Their behaviour, in public at any rate, should be predictable, if those responsible for the teaching of 'respect' had carried out their task conscientiously. But, as the Ngoni themselves recognized, it was one thing to have a system of training with a desired goal in view. It was another thing to see how each individual child responded to the training, and either conformed to the code or resisted it. The Ngoni thought that the clue to conformity or resistance lay in the individual's character, and they talked a great deal about the character of their children. Such conversations generally arose when adults were watching a group of boys and girls carrying out a socially required or self-appointed task. They might be bringing back the cattle in the evening, practising for the *ngoma* dance, grinding bulrush millet for snacks for the little children, asking each other riddles or telling a story. Some of the tasks called for intelligence, some for physical strength, some for initiative or organizing ability, some for eloquence.

Character, so the Ngoni thought, came from two sources, inborn qualities and acquired qualities. The first they called *mabadidwe*, literally those things which an individual was born with. These included physical resemblances to their parents, such as colour of skin, shape of face and features, posture and carriage, speaking voice; and the less tangible qualities such as control of temper, power to command others, eloquence in speech, as well as anti-social characteristics such as cruelty, rages, meanness, jealousy. Both kinds of inborn qualities, physical and moral, could come from either parent. In the case of the average child, who was not outstanding in any way, few comments if any were made on his heredity. But if a child showed outstanding ability or powers of leadership, or was on the contrary always quarrelling or showing off or sulking, they looked for an explanation of such qualities in his parentage.

Yet heredity was not in Ngoni thinking the only explanation for a child's character. Nor did they believe that it always followed that a cruel father had vicious sons, nor a mother who was tactful and pacific, daughters showing the same traits. They thought character, though partly inherited, was modified by and moulded by acquired qualities due to training. In the case of bad inherited qualities they could be, it was hoped, corrected by persistent training. When desirable qualities were shown by either or both parents it was always hoped that the child would also show them, and that good upbringing would ensure their development. They were always puzzled when sons of outstanding men and daughters of distinguished women turned out badly.

The acquired qualities were known as *makhalidwe*, the root of which was *kukhala*. This was a word used in a great many contexts with different meanings in each. In the context of child training it was used to mean to behave, with the added implication that it was what a person was like, due to his behaviour. *Makhalidwe* was used therefore, in the sense of conduct, implying behaviour in all relationships and including what had been acquired through response to training.

As we shall see later, Ngoni elders were afraid to leave a child, especially a girl after the age of seven or so, in her mother's household if the mother showed obvious signs of being a 'bad character'. They might take the child away and put her with some relative of acknowledged 'good character', in the hope of offsetting the effects of heredity by careful training.

In later childhood and especially on the threshold of adulthood, as we shall see in Chapters VI and VII, boys and girls were expected to learn and practise traditional Ngoni skills and to be conversant with traditional Ngoni knowledge. Skills and knowledge, or rather the ability to use them, might be inherited from a parent, but they were generally regarded as acquired qualities. In any case, they needed careful training and direction in order that they might be fully developed.

Ngoni cultural values

After the Scottish Mission had been in North Nyasaland for some time, and the Bible and other Christan literature had been translated into the vernacular, Bunyan's *Pilgrim's Progress* became one of the most popular and widely read books in Ngoniland, both by older children and by adults. The reason was that its imagery portrayed so many ideas and situations which the Ngoni recognized as being relevant for them in the new world to which they had to adapt themselves. It became for Ngoni Christians, and for many others too since it was told far more often than it was read, a new kind of folk-tale, and was told as such to children in school and in the villages. The themes of striving towards a goal, and fighting lions and giants on the way, and listening to good advice as well as hearing bad—these and other themes were recognized as in the Ngoni tradition although in such a different setting.

In the final chapter of this book we shall talk about personality and character among the Ngoni, looking at the ideas of basic personality as set out by Linton and others, and trying to see how training at different stages of childhood had been converging towards the ideal personality of the Ngoni man and woman. It will give us an opportunity of looking more closely at the values inherent in Ngoni culture and implicit in all the training of their children. I propose here only to put down a brief list of these values, in order that they may be kept in mind during the detailed narrative of the upbringing of children in the following chapters. There were three main group values which Ngoni families and village and national groups had always before them: keeping together as a people; dominating but with paternal benevolence those subject to their rule; and mutual aid and trust between the individuals in the Ngoni groups. Thus there was a strong in-group feeling of interdependence contrasted with a feeling towards the out-group of kindly but firm authority.

In the realm of personal behaviour to others, respect and obedience were always expected towards elders and superiors. Self-control, involving a high degree of restraint, was expected towards superiors, equals and inferiors. Generosity was expected of everyone towards his equals and inferiors.

A group of three qualities which showed Ngoni values were always being quoted as the distinguishing marks of 'true Ngoni' men and women: physical strength with which physical courage was closely associated; persistence and thoroughness in any task undertaken or assigned; and wisdom which was sharply contrasted with being clever, and which included knowledge, good judgement, ability to control people and keep the peace, and skill in using speech.

8. A well-filled grain store

9. Winnowing

10. Young musicians

III

'A New Stranger has come'

In these words the father's mother announced from the door of the hut that a child had been born. From inside the hut the women assisting the mother at the time of delivery had given a single cry if it was a boy and two cries for a girl. If the birth had been delayed till late afternoon towards sunset, the women in the hut said to the mother, if it was a boy: 'See the baby has been awaiting the return of the cattle, because it is he who will tend the cattle.'

The new baby was at first regarded as a stranger, born by a woman who had herself come to the village as a stranger when she married. In later years, when speaking of his parents, the child would say: 'X is my father, and I am of the womb of A, and G and H they are my brother and my sister of one womb.' This particularization of a full brother and sister was used to correct the extended use of the kinship terms, and also to convey the idea that having been born from the womb of one woman gave children a special relationship important in Ngoni thinking.

Preparation for birth

When an Ngoni wife was aware that she was pregnant she did not say anything to her husband, and indeed endeavoured to conceal her condition from him as long as possible, continuing the normal sleeping arrangements and intercourse. Ngoni women liked to assert their authority and ascendancy on those occasions, and therefore excluded the men from knowledge of the coming event and from all preparations for it. The senior women used to say, 'Men are little children. They are not able to hear those things which belong to pregnancy.' The men on their part accepted the role of being ignorant of what was coming, though they were generally aware of it. It was an elaborate piece of role-playing, standardized by custom, emphasizing the separation of the men's and women's worlds in Ngoni life, and giving control and authority into the experienced hands of the senior women.

The Ngoni culture pattern forbade the wife to tell her mother-in-law herself about her condition. She had, as so often in the Ngoni pattern, to approach first a friend who was her confidante, who might be another young wife or a helper in the household. This friend had to tell her mother-in-law, the future paternal grandmother of the baby, who was destined to play a big part in the child's upbringing.

During the months of pregnancy a Ngoni woman carried on with her normal work in the household, including cooking for her husband. If she feared a miscarriage, and suffered from what was called 'a shaking inside', she stayed quietly in the hut, and, saying that she had a headache, asked her husband to call her friend. Then the friend told the mother-in-law who sent for a 'doctor' to bring medicines 'to make the inside not shake'. A young Ngoni woman did not expect to have miscarriages, and feared that her husband's relatives would blame her home for not giving her enough food before marriage to make her strong and healthy in child-bearing.

The fear of invidious comparisons with her own home and upbringing also operated when the wife felt herself near to labour. She would keep on working up to the last minute, for if she told her friend that her time was come, and the friend summoned the senior women, they came to examine her. Should they find on examination that she was not about to deliver, they looked at her and said, 'What are you afraid of? Did you call us for fear?' The young wife was ashamed of being thought fearful, both for her own reputation and because it was implied that her family had not given her good instruction and advice before marriage.

The birth of the child

When the senior women were satisfied that labour was about to begin, they took charge of all the preparations. They first sent out of the hut all the things belonging to the husband, his clothes, axes, spears, shields, and all the good mats, pots and baskets. Only old mats and clothes and pots were used during labour, and the hut was henceforth unclean and forbidden to the husband and to all males. The mother-in-law directed operations, with the help of her co-wives, the wives of her husband's brothers, widowed sisters of her husband, and some of the wives of the younger generation. The women who took an active part in the actual delivery were the older ones, but several younger women came to assist, or look on, and to encourage the young wife.

She was made to sit on a mat leaning back against the knees of another woman, and the experienced 'midwives' were in front to receive the child in their hands. She was told to bear down and sometimes given a bark rope tied to the rafters to pull on. Though she might be in great pain, she was not expected to cry out or even to groan. The older women talked to her encouragingly, and wiped her face, or gave her a little water to drink. After the birth, the woman knelt forward leaning on her hands until the placenta was born. It was buried in a hole, in the floor at the back of the hut on the women's side.

The baby was washed by a senior woman and oiled with castor oil. The cord was tied with thread and the baby was given very thin gruel made of finger millet fried and ground. This was intended to act as a purgative to get rid of the mucus in the stomach. After this had been ejected, a tiny bit of the sour milk curds was put in the baby's mouth.

The mother was washed and covered with a cloth and left to rest, while the women folded up the delivery mat ready for burning, and generally cleaned up. The fire in the middle of the hut was rekindled to warm the mother and baby, and gruel was given to the mother of millet flour, brought from the mother-in-law's hut where it had been cooked. With the help of the other women, the mother washed her breasts with warm water and massaged them to make the milk flow, ready for the child to suck.

The other ethnic groups surrounding the Ngoni in Nyasa-land considered it disastrous if a child was born face down or with the buttocks first, and twins were dreaded as ill omens. The Ngoni shared none of these beliefs and were particularly considerate for the mother of twins, often killing a beast to give the mother meat and broth to increase her flow of milk. The only notice the Ngoni took of the method of presentation at birth was that they gave a child a name indicative of such a birth. They gave special names for the first and second twin born. If one twin died it was buried under the veranda of the hut and a smooth stone was placed on top. This stone was used for sitting on, and the surviving twin was held on it when being washed.

Ritual and social uncleanness

From the time just before the birth took place the hut and everything in it, and the woman and her new baby, were considered ritually unclean. If she had to leave the hut to answer the call of nature, she covered herself with a cloth from head to foot and avoided meeting anyone. She did no cooking herself until the ritual uncleanness was removed. Food was brought to her from her mother-in-law's hut or from her co-wives' huts, a special dish was used and washed separately, and she did not use her hands to eat with but a wooden spoon which was also washed separately. During the period of seclusion within the hut one of the senior women who helped at the birth slept in the hut with the mother and baby. No other young children were allowed to sleep in the hut, though they might come in to see the baby. All males over the age of ten had to avoid the hut and its inhabitants altogether. The husband slept either in the boys' dormitory or with the husband of the woman who was looking after his wife.

This ritual uncleanness extended to any food once it was carried into the hut. Ngoni women used to demonstrate their love for their husbands by stopping cooked food being carried into the hut, and sending it instead by the child who brought it to her husband where the men were gathered at the gate of the kraal.

Ritual cleansing of a hut and its occupants took place in stages. At the time of 'bringing out the child', which I shall shortly describe, the hut itself was made clean again. It was thoroughly swept, and the floor and veranda were smeared with cowdung. Cowdung was used habitually for smearing on floors, prior to polishing them with a smooth stone. But fresh wet cowdung rubbed on the hands was also used for ritual cleansing after some 'dangerous' act such as touching sacred objects or administering the royal medicines. In the case of its use after childbirth it was undoubtedly used in the ritual sense, for the operation was called 'making the hut safe for the husband to sleep in'. The household goods were then put back in their places, anyone could go into the hut, and the husband returned to sleep there, though on a separate mat on his, the right-hand side, of the fireplace. If the child was a first baby, the husband's return to sleep in the hut was delayed, since the senior women stayed on to instruct the young mother how to take care of the baby at night, and especially how to be careful not to smother it as it lay beside her on her mat.

'Coming out of the hut'

The falling of the cord was the signal that the baby was ready to 'come out of the hut' and be presented to the village. Ngoni women used to hasten the falling of the cord by burning a maize cob, and squeezing into the ashes the juice of the small bitter thorn apple and mixing in castor oil. This was applied with a feather to the baby's navel.

When the cord dropped the baby's head was shaved, and the mother shaved a little hair round her temples. Then they washed carefully, using sweet-smelling soapy leaves, oiled the baby's skin, put on clean clothes, and came out of the hut door and sat on a clean mat outside. This first public coming out of the hut took place in the late afternoon, so that the men, after their work was finished, could come to 'salute the new stranger'. The husband and his brothers were the first to come, and this was the first time he had seen the baby. They brought small presents such as a fowl or a basket of flour, and always strings of beads which were tied round the baby's wrists and ankles, neck and waist. The word used for these little gifts was 'to give a present just for pleasing', and Ngoni Christians when speaking of such presents to new babies likened them to the gifts brought by the Magi to the infant Christ.

While the husband and his immediate kinsmen came to greet the baby at the hut door, the senior men of the village stayed by the gate of the kraal. After the cattle had come back that evening and the kraal gates were shut, the grand-mother carried the baby to the gate and presented him to the senior men who responded by giving small presents to the child. This was always done if the baby was a boy, but sometimes omitted for girls.

When small children seeing the new baby on its mother's lap asked where it came from, they were always told that the mother had found it by the river in the rushes on the bank. The object of this reply, so Ngoni women said, was to hide the secret of birth from the children and stop them asking further questions. The Ngoni culture pattern of child-hood innocence required that children should be kept in ignorance of birth and sexual intercourse while they were young. By adults therefore they were put off with stories of finding the baby on the river bank. As usual, however, in societies maintaining officially a conspiracy of silence, the stories were only standard replies by adults to children, and most adults admitted that children pursued these inquiries among themselves and found out what they wanted to know from each other.

Naming the child

After coming out of the hut and being presented to its male kin and to the elders of the village as 'the new stranger', the baby was given a name. The choice of a name was usually left to the baby's paternal grandfather. He sometimes gave it his name or his father's name, if a boy, or if a girl, his mother's name or his father's sister's name. There was no ceremony attached to naming. After the matter had been talked over by the men at the kraal gate, the grandfather came to the hut, and called the mother and child out and said, 'His name is so and so.' The personal name was seldom used in ordinary social intercourse, but in spite of this every child was given a personal name, and sometimes had added to it a descriptive name indicating that it had been born face downwards, or born a twin, or born too soon after the previous baby.

At this time of naming, the father, or more generally the paternal grandfather, prepared a 'carrying skin' for the mother to carry the baby in. It really belonged to the baby rather than to the mother, for it was used by the nurse girl to carry the baby, and she had the child in her charge most of the day. The skin was that of a goat or small calf from the herd owned by the house to which the baby's father belonged. The skin was cleaned and scraped and made soft by rubbing in fat, and handed over to the mother with some of the meat for broth, and the rest of the meat was eaten by the males of that house. The gift in time became a cloth and not a skin, as skins for wearing or household use went out of fashion. The cloth when presented however was still called a 'carrying skin' and a goat or a calf from the herd of the house was still killed and eaten. The cloth came out of the store of cloth bought when cattle were sold, and kept in the hut of the senior woman of the father's house.

Visit to the mother's home

If, as was always the case in earlier days, the mother of the new baby had come from a distant village, she did not see her own mother or her relatives, and they did not see the child until it was several weeks old, and considered by the senior women strong enough to undertake a journey. Then a visit involving much ceremony took place, for the wife's mother-in-law headed the party. The stiff and formal relations between the two sets of 'in-laws' had been eased slightly through the series of feasts and exchanges which preceded and followed the marriage ceremony. Face-to-face intercourse was, however, still very formal between the two families, and this first visit with the grandchild was in one sense an act of condescension on the part of the husband's family, since the child belonged to them. It was also a human and natural recognition of the eagerness of the young mother to see her own mother and display her child. Word was sent in advance by a messenger from the husband's village to announce the visit, so that the wife's family could make due preparation.

The main object of this visit was, in the Ngoni phrase, 'to show the child at its mother's home'. The young mother and baby, with her mother-in-law in the place of honour, sat outside the big house of the girl's father's family. Her father and his male relatives came to salute the child and to give it presents of beads, and in modern times small gifts of money as well. If the girl's father owned many cattle, he killed a beast, and they feasted that night, and the visitors carried home meat with them as well as the presents to the child. It was all very formal and correct, except when the young mother escaped for a short time to the circle of her sisters and girlhood friends, and exchanged confidences with them.

56

After this formal visit had taken place, the young mother was free to visit her former home more often, and her relatives could come and see her and her baby in her husband's village.

Taking care of the baby

There were two special features of infant care among the Ngoni which were not found among the neighbouring peoples. One was the assignment of a nurse girl from outside the circle of relatives to care for a new infant. The nurse girl was chosen by the grandmother from among her dependent household staff, and was allotted to one particular baby. The girl, who was usually in her early teens and unmarried, was supervised by an older woman, also of the grandmother's household. This woman watched over the personal behaviour of several nurse girls, as well as seeing that they did their work properly as nurses.

The nurse girl took charge of the baby in the early morning and kept it with her all day until nightfall, bringing it back to the mother at more or less regular intervals for suckling. The mother played with the baby if she felt like it, and sent for the nurse girl to bring it to her if strangers came and she wanted to display the child. The Ngoni commended this practice by saying that their women kept clean because they did not carry babies about all day on their backs. They admitted at the same time that many infants grew greatly attached to their nurse girls, to the extent of being happier with them than with their mother. The nurse girls did not take little babies far afield. They stayed around within the fences of the household or near at hand, helping with domestic chores, chatting to other nurse girls, helping to prepare meals, and eating with the baby's mother and anyone else who formed part of the household eating unit. At night, after she had given the baby to its mother, she went off to sleep in the hut of the older woman who was in charge of her and other nurse girls.

57

When the baby cried, and it was not time to take him to his mother for suckling, the nurse girl jogged him up and down on her back, and walked to and fro with him endlessly, crooning little lullabies to soothe the baby. Some of these lullabies were traditional, handed down from the older women, others were improvised by a nurse girl or copied by her from another.

Two traditional lullabies, well know in the Northern Ngoni kingdom, were as follows:

> *Hush my child;*
> *Never mind, never mind,*
> *Hush my child;*
> *Never mind, never mind,*
> *There is a busybody gossiping*
> *There is a busybody gossiping*
> *Ho! We reap the maize*

> *Kholwane, Kholwane, son of Makhwaphuna,*
> *What are you carrying?*
> *I am carrying the food of the baby*
> *For someone may go about defiling it*
> *In the dark paths.*

The following is an example of an impromptu lullaby which I heard from a nurse girl in the Northern kingdom:

> *Bu, bu, bu, bu,*
> *The baby cries for its nurse and not for its mother.*
> *Bu, bu, bu, bu,*
> *She is coming to make gruel for the baby.*
> *There she comes,*
> *Bu, bu, bu, bu;*
> *The baby sleeps.*

The reference to the baby's food in two of the lullabies belongs to the second special feature of Ngoni infant care, the provision of baby food to supplement the mother's milk, and the arrangements for artificial feeding if the mother had not enough milk, or was unable to suckle the child, or was ill or died. If a woman died in or just after childbirth, and the child survived, it might be suckled by the paternal grandmother or by another co-wife of the dead woman, but as a rule they resorted to artificial feeding, and often used it to supplement breast feeding. The father of the child took the food pipe of a beast recently killed, washed it and dried it, and handed it over to the women to rub with fat until it was soft and pliable. One end was then tied tightly to close it, it was filled with warm cow's milk, and the other end was tied loosely so that the child could just suck through it. It was kept well washed with warm water, and many infants were brought up successfully with this 'bottle'.

The babies were also given very thin gruel made of millet or maize flour, and curds and whey beaten up together. This was put in a very small gourd, decorated with drawings, with a spout to pour from, and a cover to keep flies and dust out.

Weaning

Studies of weaning in different cultures lay emphasis on the traumatic shock of separation from the mother, not only in terms of being refused the breast, but also of being removed to sleep elsewhere than beside the mother, and perhaps being sent away to stay with another relative.

In the Ngoni pattern of nurse-girl care and of supplementary feeding, especially after the first few months, it might seem that the actual weaning was less of a shock than in cultural situations where the baby was with the mother all day, carried about by her and never refused the breast if it cried. Ngoni women, however, and men too, all asserted that weaning was a shock to the child, even if it happened at two years old.

The reasons for this shock were partly that it was done all in one morning at one fell swoop, and partly that the child was sent away from the mother at night. The same nurse girl looked after it all day, but now took it more often to other compounds, so that the child should not 'see the mother's breasts and cry for them'. Nevertheless they did cry, some of them day and night at first, and many for weeks at night when the indulgent warmth of the mother on her mat was exchanged for the kindly but somewhat stern care of the grandmother or another older woman. Paternal grandmothers did not believe in spoiling Ngoni children, and the child was often left to cry itself to sleep.

The Ngoni used to say: 'On the day when a child was weaned, all the village knew. It was not a secret. People spoke about it to show that the parents were now free to have another child.' The mother-in-law and the other senior women of the father's family took the initiative as well as assuming responsibility for deciding the moment for weaning. Those same senior women who had assisted at the birth of the child arrived one morning on the veranda of the mother's hut and announced, 'We want to wean this child.' Apparently the mother was sometimes capable of refusing to co-operate. She did not want to give up suckling the child, so she picked it up and ran out of the hut past the women, and hid herself and her child with some of her friends. The senior women did not stoop to argument. They formed into a procession and filed out of the compound saying, 'Well, she has refused. She can now find the proper time herself, with her husband.' The young mother, who had yielded to a sudden impulse, found herself on reflection in great difficulty. It was considered a 'shame' for her to do the weaning herself, and her husband was jeered at by his brothers and friends for having a rebellious wife who did not pay attention to the claims of his family on the child.

So when the senior women announced that they had come to do the weaning, most young mothers meekly submitted, whatever their personal sentiments were. The senior women pounded chillies and put the hot paste on the mother's breasts, and held the child near enough to smell the chillies, even to touch them. They said to the child, 'Leave it alone.

This breast is now bad'—and they spat downwards as they did when something was really bad. While the child was howling with fright and frustration, the mother's breasts were covered with a cloth. The child was then picked up and carried away in its carrying cloth to the compound of its paternal grandmother, or a widowed paternal aunt, attended by its own nurse girl. If it had a feeding bottle, or one could be made for it, it was given cow's milk, as well as gruel, and curds and whey. The Ngoni women believed that if a weaned child was given cow's milk it would forget its mother's breasts quickly, but they admitted that it was a conventional belief and not always justified.

Social relationships involved in the birth of a child: Wife to husband's family

Throughout the period of pregnancy, during childbirth and after, up to and including weaning, the mother of a new baby was made to feel her position as a stranger among her husband's relatives. Before marriage it had been impressed on her by her own family that, at any rate in the early years of marriage, she must be obedient and humble, not only to establish her own present and future position among her husband's people, but for the sake of the reputation of her own family from whom she was now separated. The key relationship in this cycle of pregnancy, birth, weaning and new conception was that between her and her mother-in-law. If she showed respect by being humble and obedient, she could establish a behaviour pattern which in the end reward-ed her by giving her self-respect because she was doing her duty in accepting the authority of her husband's mother. It was no easy path for a high-spirited girl who had had freedom and indulgence in her own home. She knew however that these first few years of marriage and child-bearing were the critical ones. She could see for herself how women who had been married longer had more freedom from the authority of their mothers-in-law because they had learned how to handle them, as well as how to conform to required behaviour. So she put up with present restrictions for the sake of future peace and harmony. Her lot was to live there with her husband's people, and the birth of the child was a strong link in the chain which bound her to them. Meantime she found some relief in her friends among the other young wives, and particularly with the one in whom she placed her confidence, and who acted as her go-between with her mother-in-law.

Wife to husband

Throughout the intricate and often vexing relations with her mother-in-law and other senior women, the husband-wife relationship remained for the young mother a steadying and constant factor. She had been attracted to him in courtship; she had had the chance of accepting or refusing him when the marriage proposals were made; the cattle had been handed over to her father to seal the marriage contract. For all these and other reasons she held on to her love for her husband and her relationship with him, whatever overbearing behaviour might be shown her by his relatives. Hence she took care of his possessions in the hut they shared, helping the senior women to send them out of the hut just before the confinement. She redirected food towards him when it was sent to her during her confinement, gladly going short herself in order to prove her devotion. She was glad that after coming out of the hut, having a nurse girl meant that she could keep her body and her clothes clean and sweet-smelling and therefore pleasing to him. She was happy when the ritual cleansing of the hut and of herself made it possible for her to cook for her husband again and endear him to her by that means. When weaning the child caused her pain and frustration, there was at the same time a deep satisfaction that full intercourse was now officially permitted between her and her husband, and that they were free to have another child.

62

Father's family to child

Ngoni children were indeed the children of their fathers from the time of their birth onwards. They were born into a 'house', of which their father was a member. If their father divorced his wife or she ran away, the children remained in the custody of his family. We have seen how the paternal grandmother took charge of all the preparations for birth, and of the actual birth itself. It was her proud duty to present the child to the public after the 'coming out of the hut' ceremony, when she took it to the kraal gate where the assembled elders were sitting. The other senior women of Ngoni families held her responsible for advising on the spacing between the birth of this new baby and the next, so that the interests of this child should be safeguarded. If it was suspected that the young wife was pregnant again before the grandmother had planned to wean the child, the other senior women said to her: 'Look now. You are foolish. The child has been endangered. You are like an enemy to him.' That touched her on a very vital point, and she in turn accused the young parents of harming the present child. Having rebuked them, generally in public, she followed it up with a box on the ear for her son and his wife. When this next child was born it was called 'the destroyer', because by following on too quickly, it had injured the propects of the first child.

Baby to nurse girl and women helpers

The baby, as we have seen, spent a great deal of its time in the company of its nurse girl, and after weaning she was its constant companion. She and the older woman helpers who supervised her formed a counterbalancing influence to the paternal grandmother, though outwardly they obeyed her instructions about the care of the child. The nurse girl especially was inclined to be indulgent; she was young and playful; the baby was her only responsibility. She was anxious to protect her charge in every way, and with the connivance of the women helpers she made little charms of bits of roots to hang around the baby's neck to make him grow quickly and to ward off sorcery and witchcraft. She threaded pumpkin seeds and tied them around his neck to make his teeth come quickly if they were late in appearing. These charms were generally those used by the local peoples, and Ngoni fathers were contemptuous about their use and efficacy. 'These women are spoiling our children,' they said, and then reassured themselves by remembering that a boy would be free from such women's spoiling once he went into the boys' dormitory.

Variants on the Ngoni pattern

This traditional pattern of authority and behaviour in respect of birth, infant care and weaning was essentially that of the true Ngoni, that relatively small aristocratic group who never forgot their superior social status and its foundation in their ancestry. This first stage in the socialization of a child, from birth to weaning, brought out clearly two fundamental features of Ngoni social organization. One was the role played by the senior women who had themselves in their childhood been brought up on strict Ngoni lines. The father of the new baby accepted the role played by his own mother in controlling, and if necessary coercing, his young wife. Though, as we shall see later, every Ngoni boy and young man had a period of virtually complete escape from feminine control, once a man married and his young wife was established within the social group of his mother's house, he acknowledged his mother's authority over her, and particularly over the birth and care of his child. The mother-son relationship of the young father to his own mother dominated the relationship of the young mother to her child. Young Ngoni fathers never questioned their allegiance to their own mothers, cherishing them as they grew older and supporting them in their exercise of authority. Much as he loved his

11. Young
musicians

12.   Chiefs' wives wearing leopard claws

13.   Chiefs' wives leading in the dance

young wife, an Ngoni husband would not normally support her against his own mother. In the case of his child, who was born a member of his family, house and clan, his mother and her circle of senior women had uncontested sway.

The second features of Ngoni social organization which the 'arrival of a new stranger' demonstrated was the women's interest in and capacity for planning and organization. The senior women had no doubt about what steps to take and who should take them, from the time when labour began till after weaning. The preparations for the birth, the receiving of the child, the care of mother and baby after birth, the ritual cleansing of the hut, the presentation of the child to the public—all these acts up to and including weaning were planned with what seemed an elaborate organization when first observed, but which turned out to be standard Ngoni practice. Two particular aspects of this organization stood out as different from the local practices: the provision for artificial feeding of the child, and the role played by nurse girls and women helpers.

The main variants in this pattern arose from three causes: the effect of marriage with women of other ethnic groups who married into Ngoni families and had to accept the pattern of authority imposed by the house organization of Ngoni women. They therefore had to follow in its main lines the procedures we have described for the birth and care of infants. But Ngoni men and women deplored in particular two non-Ngoni elements which were creeping into the conduct of birth and post-natal ceremonies. One was the attitude taken during difficult labour when the women attending to the mother tried to force her to confess to illicit sexual relations which the non-Ngoni believed to be the cause of the delayed birth. The other was the prohibition on a wife putting salt in the food she was cooking while she was menstruating or at any other ritually unclean period. The true Ngoni despised this salt taboo and the women of Ngoni families did not practise it.

Changes in residence at and after marriage influenced the composition of the group of relatives who assisted at births. In the central kingdom daughters of leading men in the village often stayed in their father's village at marriage. Hence the father's sisters were often present at the birth and the wife's mother and her sisters might be living in the village. If the wife belonged to a higher ranking Ngoni clan than her husband, her relatives shared responsibility with those of the husband's family.

As may be imagined the struggle between mother-in-law control and western medical practices at childbirth was a protracted one. Even when there was a younger member of the husband's family trained as a nurse or midwife, she by no means had her way in organizing the conduct of the birth. She might introduce a few hygienic measures such as clean cloths instead of old rags, and sterilized thread for tying the cord. But unless the senior women were frightened, and they seldom were, by prolonged and difficult labour, the Ngoni families were averse to taking a young mother into hospital. The chief reason was the challenge to the authority of the mother-in-law, especially when the younger women who had some knowledge of western medical practices questioned the advice of the senior women.

IV

Family Life for the Young Child

The women's world

It was the proud boast of the Ngoni aristocrats that their women did no 'work' in the old days. When they spoke thus they were equating 'work' with physical labour, sweeping and cleaning in the hut and compound, fetching wood and water, hoeing in the gardens, and the routine part of preparing and cooking food. The Ngoni women of the former large households had an army of 'helpers' to do all these tasks for them. Though the number of helpers dwindled as the larger households disappeared, the pattern of appropriation of tasks remained in the shrunken households, and hence the Ngoni women were always responsible for a high degree of household management. Larger households in the old days fed fifty to sixty people from their cooking-pots, and though when I lived among them the scale of their households was much smaller, some were still feeding twenty and more people for each meal, apart from the occasional meals served when kinsfolk and strangers came unexpectedly.

I never failed to be impressed with the quiet dignified competence with which Ngoni women managed their household affairs. They did it with an apparent effortlessness, which had its roots in long training and tradition, and in an awareness of responsibility that increased, but weighed less heavily, with age and experience. This competence was always apparent on occasions such as wedding feasts. Then cereal food, meat, vegetable relishes were cooked in vast quantities and served out to the separate groups of guests.

These skills of management, and of order and dignity in serving, were not however only seen in large-scale operations. The modern young Ngoni wife serving tea and 'scones' to her husband's guests sitting on his veranda showed the same qualities of careful preparation and considerate service as her grandmother had shown presiding over 500 guests at a wedding feast.

Household management in Ngoni homes included primarily managing the household staff, allotting their tasks to them, settling their quarrels, looking after them when sick, marrying off the young ones when the time came. In the all-important aspect of feeding a large household and its dependents, Ngoni women assumed responsibility for seeing that there were enough supplies of different kinds of food at hand, for regular consumption and for emergencies. They consulted at times with the 'official' who was in charge of their 'house' about mobilizing supplies or organizing women helpers to cultivate in the gardens. Most significant in the eyes of Ngoni and non-Ngoni alike was the task of Ngoni women of 'dividing the food' at every meal-time. It was a key concept in Ngoni culture that at all times when food, beer, or other kinds of goods were to be divided out, and enjoyed or used by a large number of people, the 'one who divided' was an important individual. He, or more often she, must be of 'good character', who assumed, or was given, the task because he or she knew how to do it, and no one questioned the justice or the competence with which the dividing was done. Again I was impressed by the almost nonchalant air with which Ngoni women ladled out food for a large number of individuals and groups. It looked so easy. It was obviously not a simple matter. The results were always accepted and welcomed, and I never heard any grumbles.

Central to the organization of the household, and in one sense the axis on which it revolved, was the care and attention the wife gave to her husband. Cooking, including the choice and variety of food, was primarily to please him, and to meet the incessant claims on his hospitality when visitors came. A well-ordered and harmonious household also pleased him, and conversely the sounds of women quarrelling angered him and violated his canons of accepted Ngoni behaviour. It was his wife's task to supervise the household helpers, who were mostly non-Ngoni, and to make them conform to Ngoni patterns by controlling their rages, instead of yelling at each other and hurling accusations of witchcraft at those with whom they were angry.

Ngoni women also took a serious view of another aspect of pleasing their husbands, namely attention to their person and dress. The old elaborate hair-dressing of Ngoni women, the scrupulous washing of their bodies with sweet-smelling leaves, the use of oil and clarified butter on the skin and hair, and the careful tying and draping of cloths and arranging of bead headbands and necklaces—these all were forms of beauty treatment and personal hygiene designed to please the husband. They also reinforced the self-respect and authority of well-born Ngoni women, marking them out by their well-groomed appearance from the 'workers' and 'helpers' who surrounded them.

The young Ngoni child, up to the age of six or seven, grew up in a women's world of the kind just described. His mother was learning from his paternal grandmother the increasing duties and responsibilities of an Ngoni wife, although she was supposed to have learned some of them in her own home from her mother before marriage. We saw in Chapter II how the social horizons of a small Ngoni child were never of a narrow type, restricted to his individual family. The care of a child, especially between the time of weaning and the coming of second teeth, was the concern of a number of women in addition to his own mother, from whom he was snatched away at weaning, and, for a time at least, kept away from her household for eating and sleeping.

Among the female population of a village most nearly

related to a young child by kinship, there were three distinct age-groups. Nearest in age to him were his older sisters, children of his own mother, of his father's other wives, and of his father's brothers' wives. When he began to talk he addressed all these as 'sister', or rather as 'my sister', and they took a kindly interest in him, especially if he were a boy and therefore to be removed from them when the time came for him to live in the boys' dormitory. They played with him, they sometimes carried him about while the nurse girl did something else, they ground bulrush millet or roasted ground-nuts to give him as snacks. They were particularly concerned with teaching him to speak correctly, to say the right names for things, to use the correct terms for older people, and later to sing the refrains of little songs in their singing games.

Above this sister group in age came his own mother and his other 'mothers', who were his father's other wives and his father's brothers' wives. All of them he was taught to address as 'my mother'. His father's sisters on the other hand, who took a special interest in his upbringing, he addressed as 'woman father', and the name implied some measure of the authority which his father and his father's brothers exercised in the household and in the village.

Above this generation of mothers and woman-fathers came the grandmothers. Pre-eminent in supervising his life and the care taken of him was his father's own mother, but he also addressed as 'grandmother' his grandfather's other wives and his grandfather's brothers' wives.

The same triple grouping by age and generation, which the child learned by degrees to distinguish among his own kin, was repeated among the 'helpers' in his mother's and grandmother's households. There were young children who were the children of the household staff. His nurse girl and her fellow nurse girls formed a slightly senior group in this division, both by reason of their responsibilities as well as of their age. Above them, as the next generation, were the women helpers of his mother's age, one or two of whom had come with her at her marriage to attend her, and who themselves had married in her new village. Above them again were the older women helpers of his grandmother's generation, themselves grandmothers, whom he addressed as 'grandmother', as he did his own grandparents.

There were other sets of people whom the young child saw less often. When he visited his mother's relatives in her old home, he enjoyed all the allurement a child feels for living in a different place among people who want to gratify his every wish. Sometimes the maternal relatives visited the child's home, but then their relationship with him was on more formal terms. They did not dare for example to give him titbits in private, or to pet him, or even to correct him, lest his father's relatives might notice and remind them: 'This is *our* child.'

Other strangers came and went all the time, and the child learned to distinguish between the village inhabitants and those he, and others, designated as 'strangers'. He saw mostly the women who were entertained in the compound of his grandmother. He was sometimes taken by his mother when she went to greet strangers by the big house, and he learned early that he was not expected to make a noise or call attention to himself in the presence of these strangers.

In this women's world the higher age-group in each status group, that is of relatives and helpers, carried the chief authority, gave orders, and rebuked all below them for breaches of etiquette or failure to carry out commands. For the small child, the whole superstructure of authority in the women's world built round his daily life a sense of security, partly because it was so ordered and so little variable. When the Ngoni said, 'A child belongs to all the village. They can all cherish him and correct him,' they really meant this women's world, organized through the households and the families and the houses. The child's needs for food and sleep, washing and warmth, care when sick, were taken care of primarily within his mother's household, but also, and especially immediately after weaning, in his grandmother's household. His needs for food and warmth could in fact be met in any of the households which formed part of his father's house and family group. There was no greater contrast for the small boy about the age of seven between this kind of life in the women's compound and his plunge into the life of the boys' dormitory.

The father's role with young children

During day-time in Ngoni villages Ngoni men and women lived almost in two separate worlds, the women in their compounds, the men by the kraal gate or about the village. When important visitors arrived the veranda of the 'big house' became a general meeting-place. Chiefs and leading men who had acquired chairs, among other modern household furniture, preferred to entertain their guests on their own veranda where they had some degree of privacy, and to offer them chairs to sit on instead of the kraal fence to lean against. This use of chairs which they found more comfortable to sit on brought many of the fathers of families back to their own verandas now and then during the day, though they continued to eat their meals with the other men at the kraal gate, and to go there to discuss village affairs and watch over the coming and going of the cattle.

This change of habit brought the fathers of families into closer touch with their young children, and it was accelerated by the growing Christian tradition in which fathers were more closely associated with certain aspects of their children's upbringing. It was the father who arranged for the baptism of the children which took place in the local church and was a ceremony attended by most of the village, whether Christians or not. When an evangelist or a school-teacher conducted evening prayers, as they often did near the kraal where anyone could come after the evening meal, Christian fathers sometimes carried a child in their arms to the prayers.

It was the fathers who decided at what age a child should go to school, and having once enrolled the boy or girl and paid the fees, the fathers insisted on regular attendance.

All Ngoni fathers showed affection for their young children, some consistently and others when it occurred to them. They picked them up and carried them about, held their hand while they tried their first steps, listened to their attempts to speak correctly, held them in their arms when they sat on the veranda. In one village twin boys aged four were devoted to their father and he to them. When he walked about, he held a hand of each. When he sat on the veranda they were always beside him and he had an arm round each. When he was elsewhere, the twins wandered about the compound disconsolately, hand in hand, rejecting the advances of their nurse girls and uncertain what to do until he appeared again.

Ngoni fathers had to be consulted in cases of sickness when the grandmother's remedies had failed and specialist help was needed. Then the father and his brothers and their father decided whether to summon a diviner or a herbalist, and arranged for the throwing of lots or the search for 'medicines', and paid the agreed fee when the cure worked.

It was part of Ngoni tradition to keep the knowledge of death away from young children. The father was held responsible for seeing that his children were kept away from the hut where the corpse was awaiting burial, and from the funeral itself. When men and women of leading Ngoni families were buried at the edge of the kraal, and the fence enlarged so that the cattle stamped over the grave, the explanation given (though it was not the only reason) was that 'the young children should not know or fear death in this village'.

The physical surroundings of the small child

The two diagrams, overleaf, illustrate the layout of the hut and compound in typical Ngoni households. Some of these

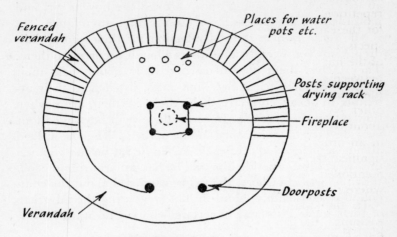

Fenced verandah

Places for water pots etc.

Posts supporting drying rack

Fireplace

Verandah

Doorposts

DIAGRAM OF HUT

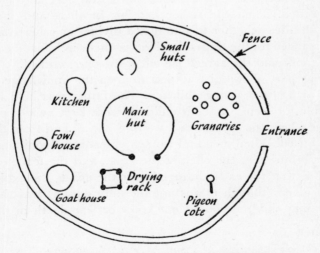

Fence

Small huts

Kitchen

Main hut

Granaries

Entrance

Fowl house

Drying rack

Goat house

Pigeon cote

DIAGRAM OF HOUSEHOLD COMPOUND

surroundings were described in Chapter I, but in spite of some repetition I have given a fuller description here to set the stage for the earlier years of a young Ngoni child. In several respects a casual observer, looking at the external appearance of the hut and the objects round it, might fail to distinguish between them and almost any Nyasaland village. Many of the household objects were indeed the same as those used by other Nyasaland peoples. But there was more elaboration about Ngoni huts and compounds; they were as a rule kept in an orderly and clean condition; and there was cultural significance about some of the features of Ngoni households mentioned here and in Chapter I which was not found elsewhere.

To the small child taken to his grandmother's hut at weaning, the space within the fence of her compound was full of interest. There was the hut itself which might be the 'great hut' of the village or one of those known as the 'right hand' and 'left hand' huts. It was generally circular, with interior walls some seven to eight feet high, with a conical roof of tightly packed grass neatly trimmed at the edges and decorated with cows' horns from the peak downwards in four lines. Inside the hut framing the doorway were the two main door-posts, solid and polished with much handling. Four posts in the middle of the floor went up to the rafters and supported cross-bars and a light platform on which gourds, herbs and green vegetables were dried. Under this platform, in the centre of the hut, was the hollow place for the fire and the three rounded hearthstones on which pots were balanced when cooking took place there. Against the back wall of the hut was a slightly raised platform in which were several small hollows for the round bottomed pots holding water, or grain or beans. Surrounding the entire hut was a raised veranda some four to five feet wide, shaded by the projecting roof, and generally fenced in all round the back, thus making extra storage space. All round the front of the hut was a well-swept space, mudded and polished in

old Ngoni families, and shining like marble, as did the hut
and veranda floors. On this polished space, or else on the
veranda, the child's grandmother sat when callers had been
announced, and from that vantage-point she could command
the entrance through the surrounding fence, and agree to
receive callers who had asked for admittance. Also in front
of the hut was another drying platform which was large
enough to offer shelter from the sun in hot weather; the
dovecot where the 'royal pigeons' lived if the household was
of the royal clan or distinguished enough to aspire to keeping pigeons. Off to one side was a hut for the goats at night
and another, hoisted up on a platform, for the poultry. On
the other side of the main hut were the grain stores, built up
on low platforms. The maize stores were up to ten feet high
and ten feet in diameter in these big households, and well-to-
do women would have four or five of them bulging with
maize cobs. There were smaller circular mudded bins for
ground-nuts and millet. Behind the hut were two or three
small huts where some of the helpers slept, and one of them
was generally a kitchen hut. Piles of wood, and bundles of
thatching grass bound neatly with bark rope, were stacked
against the fence.

There were innumerable objects around the compound of
interest to the small child prowling about. Two or three tall
wooden pounding mortars, so heavy that they could not
be lifted and had to be trundled on their circular base from
one place to another, stood near the kitchen hut, or were
moved to the front if the women pounding had to watch
children there. There were much smaller mortars for pounding ground-nuts, kept when not in use in the fenced-in
veranda; and one or more large flat stones for grinding finger
millet and bulrush millet. Baskets were of all sizes and shapes
from the small round food basket with a lid in which father's
food was carried to the kraal gate, to the wide shallow winnowing baskets, the deep round carrying baskets some as
large as two feet in diameter, and the porous baskets used as

sieves for straining beer or water poured through ashes to make salt. These lay around all day if they were being used, and were periodically scrubbed and put on the rack to dry, and at night stacked tidily in the veranda. In the day-time sleeping-mats of finely woven fibre were brought out into the sun, and so were skins and cloths used as coverings at night. Some of the Ngoni used curved wooden headrests as pillows often carved at the ends with animals' heads to fascinate a small child.

On the polished space in front of the hut were laid from time to time mats on which sprouting millet for making beer was dried, or partly pounded damp maize. A young child was sometimes told to keep the fowls and dogs off these mats. These animals and often small kids, wandered and pecked and scratched and quarrelled inside the fence all day, and young children chased them.

Beyond the fence lay other fenced compounds grouped round the cattle kraal, and beyond the village buildings lay patches of woodland, grass pastures, cultivated 'gardens', and water-holes and streams. Going with the mother or grandmother or a nurse girl or helper to fetch water, or work in the gardens was an expedition for young children which they delighted in.

In these village surroundings there were some places forbidden to young children, who were corrected by everyone with smacks and stern reproofs until they learned to keep away. One such forbidden place was the kraal gateway where the men sat and talked and ate. No woman until she had passed the menopause was allowed to cross over in front of the gateway lest she injure the cattle. If therefore children strayed down there, younger women did not like to go and fetch them back, as the men always grumbled if women went there lest they should harm the cattle. It was nevertheless a place that had a great attraction for boys of five to seven years old, because they found their fathers there and the herd boys. The boys in this age-group of five to seven showed signs of irritation at female control, especially with this prohibition on going to the kraal gate. They escaped surveillance and ran off there now and then, only to be caught by one of the men, beaten and brought back to the compound with the remark: 'This child is not yet a herd boy. Keep him with you.'

If the village was near a roadway with traffic on it, or near a river, children were forbidden to go there without some older person with them. They were also warned not to go near fireplaces in case a burning log fell out, and to keep away from the woodpile where there might be snakes.

Training in habits

In these surroundings, diversified, orderly, and on the whole safe if forbidden places were avoided, young children's needs were attended to and they were gradually trained to look after themselves. For food, health and sleep, their primary physical needs, they had their older sisters, nurse girls, mothers, grandmothers and helpers all at hand to ensure that these needs were satisfied.

After the post-weaning months were over, and generally though not always after the next baby was born, a young child went back to eat with his mother in her compound and sleep in her hut, though a grandmother, if she had taken a special fancy to a child, might say she was going to keep him to eat and sleep with her. In his mother's compound twice a day the child watched her and her helpers preparing and cooking a meal. In due time he was called to the veranda where the food lay smoking, his hands were wiped, he was made to rinse out his mouth, and he sat down beside his mother or his nurse in a circle round the food basket. This contained the mash of cooked grain, usually maize, and beside it were the little pots of cooked 'relish', beans, peas, green vegetables, tomatoes, ground-nuts. At first someone pinched up a little lump of the mash, dipped it in a relish, and popped it into his mouth, telling him to shut his mouth and chew before he swallowed. Later he learned to do this himself, with his eyes rather anxiously on the elders, lest he should take too large a lump, or get the relish all over his hand and wrist instead of only on his finger-tips. He learned, however hungry he was, not to stuff himself, and not to eat noisily. If he smacked his lips and gulped audibly, someone in the circle might say: 'I hear the guns of the Tyandla people booming.' They all stopped eating and looked at him, and he learned that a proverb could be a veiled rebuke, and he hung his head, ashamed.

Sometimes the smaller children had cow's milk or curds and whey or thin gruel given to them in a tiny gourd between the main meal-times, and through the day nurse girls and older sisters gave them little snacks if they thought of it or if the child whimpered because it was hungry. A favourite snack was ground bulrush millet, creamy and nutty to taste. Throughout this period spent in the women's world the child did not lack food either at or between meals. As he grew more mobile and independent, he went foraging in the compounds of his other mothers and his grandmothers, especially if his own mother had gone to her garden. They always welcomed him and gave him something to go on with.

After set meals the child was made to rinse his mouth, and his hands were cleaned by his nurse girl and his face and chest washed if he had covered himself with food fragments. His nurse girl found him a 'tooth-brush twig' and frayed it for him, and taught him to use it after meals as well as in the early morning.

Washing of small children was always done in the compound. While some children squirmed and yelled when washed, others liked it. They sat grinning on the veranda while their mother or nurse splashed water over them, rubbed soapy leaves on their hair, dried them with a cloth, and rubbed cow's fat on their skin. The Ngoni children in well-ordered households shone with cleanliness till they were about six years old. Then the boys dodged these female attentions, their skin became dry and scruffy, and their hair full of dust, and many of them began to suffer from sores, itch and sore eyes. The girls however, had already begun to like a clean and shining skin for the sake of being beautiful, and their ablutions were no longer under duress.

The smallest children urinated and defecated wherever they happened to be. From the age of three or four, however, they were taught to tell someone if they wanted to defecate, and taken outside the hut. Maize cobs or soft leaves or grass were used to clean the child, and then thrown on the fire. When the child began to look after himself, he was shown how to use the left hand only when cleaning himself, and told it was 'the hand of shame, only used for bad things'. From the age of four or five small girls and boys went with their mothers and the other women to the section of the surrounding bush reserved for the women's toilet. At about the same age boys and girls were taught to withdraw from the public gaze when urinating, and to conceal themselves behind a hut or in some other hiding-place. The Ngoni were extremely prudish about all physical acts connected with evacuating or sex, and began to demand correct behaviour from children at an early age.

If a child was constipated, or had diarrhoea, or was vomiting, or had a fever or stomach-ache, the nurse girl reported it to his mother who went to tell the child's paternal grandmother. For all the range of usual childish ailments the grandmother prescribed and carried out standard treatments, such as whey used as a purgative, or very thin gruel to check diarrhoea. The Ngoni women had a number of herbal remedies which they used for themselves and their children. They also used hot poultices, cupping, and forms of massage. Only when the known household remedies failed, did the grandmother tell the child's father and he, as we have seen, took the responsibility for calling in 'specialists'.

Sleep, the little child's third major need, was sometimes well ordered and sometimes erratic. It was not considered proper for children to sleep in the same hut as their parents after the age of four or five, when they might become aware that intercourse was taking place. From this age, when the Ngoni said 'they will now begin to see things and to ask questions', they went to sleep either with a widowed grandmother or senior helper.

During the 'dark half of the month' and in the rains, most people went to bed soon after dark and little children got a long sleep. When the moon was bright, and in dry weather, the whole village was astir, walking around, dancing, talking, visiting. Little children tagged round with their older sisters or nurse girls, and if they were sleepy were either picked up and carried, or put in the hut to sleep on their mat, provided there was no fire burning into which they could fall. During the day, especially in the hot weather, children dropped off to sleep just where they were, on the veranda, under the platform, or in some other shady spot.

It was just before bedtime, in the grandmother's hut, that traditional folk-tales were told, round the last flickers of a wood fire. Sometimes a child dropped off to sleep before the story was finished. Someone either took him on her lap, or dumped him on his mat and covered him up.

This acquiring of habits, directed consciously by adults, was designed to give the child increasingly a sense of being part of a community which had certain standards of behaviour. There were, in this training, some prohibitions which a child was expected to observe as soon as he could walk and talk. The most stringent was on any form of sex play between boys and girls. To avoid any likelihood of this, little boys and girls were early encouraged to form separate play groups. The elders kept an eye particularly on the boys, and if they showed any inquisitiveness in their play about the private parts of a girl playmate, they were beaten and reproved and told: 'If you do this again, I shall tell your father.'

Many little boys and girls up to the age of four or five ran about naked, but in leading Ngoni families they wore a scrap of cloth hanging in front from a bead or grass waistband. They were all taught before that age, and most stringently after it, to sit correctly. For the little girls, this meant kneeling first and then sitting with the legs tucked on one side. They always smoothed down their scrap of cloth so that their genitals were covered. Little boys often squatted, sitting on their heels. Their correct position however, especially when eating food, was to sit with their legs crossed and the soles of their feet pressed against their thighs, and their cloth or skin apron arranged to cover their genitals.

Any rudeness in speech or action towards parents or elders was corrected at once, and the child was told: 'That is not the Ngoni way.' Studied courtesy included looking down when addressed by an elder, and as we saw in Chapter II, never walking behind a group of elders but passing in front of them, bending slightly forward and murmuring: 'I am before your eyes.'

Play places and playthings

In spite of what appeared like a somewhat restrictive régime, Ngoni children were merry and busy all their waking hours. Occasionally lack of health, or an awkward temperament, produced a child who sat around by himself, or glowered at other children, or was spiteful and vindictive. For the most part their nurse girls and older sisters paid them the attention they demanded, were always ready to provide distractions and amusements, and showed them how to use all that lay around them as playthings.

The places where they played depended on their age and mobility. The youngest children stayed round the hut and inside the fence. Occasionally the nurse girls and older sisters in the afternoons took them to a 'playground' on the outskirts of the village, where the older girls were accustomed to meet and practise dancing, or to thread beads and chatter. When the harvest was in, some of the older children about five and six years old, helped by the nurse girls, made 'play

houses' among the maize stalks, tying the stalks together to
make conical shelters. There they played house, pretending
to cook and pound. But the enthusiasm for these playhouses
was shortlived, and on the whole the children and their nurse
girls preferred to be in the village where they could see and
hear what was going on. The older boys in this age-group
seldom went to the playground, and pursued their games in
the open spaces of the village.

The small girls had 'dolls' which they treated as little
babies. Sometimes it was a maize cob tucked into a bit of
cloth and carried on their backs. More realistic dolls were
made of a bundle of reeds tied together with the hard round
shell of a fruit fitted on top and painted with eyes, nose and
mouth. Older girls made these dolls for the little ones, and
showed them how to feed the doll from a tiny gourd and
taught them lullabies to sing while they jogged the dolls on
their back or nursed them on their lap.

Little boys had a wider range of toys, made for them by
older brothers and quickly copied by the children themselves. They made windmills from maize sheaths which
twisted on a stick as they ran. They had hoops of bamboo
peelings, trundled with a notched stick, and a small round
solid wooden wheel with a hole in it which they pushed with
a long-handled crook. They had tops of wood and whipped
them with lengths of bark rope. They were for ever collecting
scraps of iron from wherever men were working. These they
sharpened on stones, and used as knives, or bound them to a
haft, as a little axe, with fragments of skin which they
scrounged when a shield was being cut, or an ox flayed. The
small boys were the tinkers of the village, collecting whatever scrap they thought they could use, and hiding it each
in his own safe and secret place, and fighting savagely if
anyone robbed a secret store. Many boys spent hours making
clay figures, men, cattle, monkeys, dogs, and there were certain conventions which allowed little variety governing their
style and shape. Sometimes they drew, or 'wrote' as they

said, in the sand more conventional figures of men and animals which are reproduced here. Their ingenuity in the use of local materials was boundless, and led later to remarkably accurate scale models of lorries and aeroplanes made from pith, bamboo and thorns.

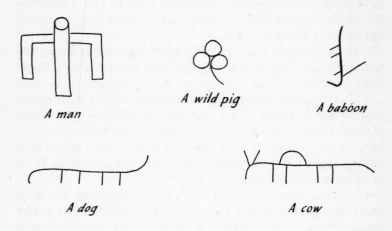

A man

A wild pig

A baboon

A dog

A cow

Most of the games such as tops and hoops were seasonal. They appeared suddenly in the village, lasted for a few weeks and then ceased as abruptly as they had begun. A perennial amusement among Ngoni boys of five to seven was playing at law courts. They sat round in traditional style with a 'chief' and his elders facing the court, the plantiffs and defendants presenting their case, and the counsellors conducting proceedings and cross-examining witnesses. In their high squeaky voices the little boys imitated their fathers whom they had seen in the courts, and they gave judgements, imposing heavy penalties, and keeping order in the court with ferocious severity. Another game which the boys of five to seven enjoyed was a form of tug-of-war, two gangs pulling on a bark rope, until one gave way, with shouting, whistling and a final cry: 'The strong ones. They prevail.'

In the dry season which was the dancing season children

from three and four years upwards spent hours watching the older boys and girls dancing. On the edge of the main group small boys particularly would with intense solemnity and exaggerated movements practise steps and postures, singing meanwhile. The Ngoni used no drums and no musical instruments in their dancing, and despised the users of drums. All their rhythm and synchrony was achieved by perfect unison of action and voice. The little boys practising solo on the edge of a dance-group listened intently every now and then to get the rhythm correctly, shifted their feet and stamped with the rest.

The little girls were collected together by older girls now and then, and sometimes joined by the boys, to play games of catch and various miming games such as choosing a lover, hen and chickens, slave-raiding, baboons in the maize gardens. These were accompanied by songs in which the leader, or 'owner', of the game sang the story and the rest joined in the refrains. Many of these miming games called for alertness and co-operation, and the slow and solitary were soon shown up and laughed at. Another set of songs with refrains were ballads or stories without action, and these were listened to by the hour by the younger children towards the end of the day, especially if the singer of the ballad was a lively narrator.

Girl children of this age-group spent a lot of their time watching adults and older girls doing their household work. In time they learned to imitate the actions of pounding and grinding, using a small pole or a stone, of sweeping with a frayed-out stalk, of winnowing or sieving with a little basket, or ladling food with a tiny wooden spoon. When they went to the gardens with their mother, they were given a small branch to carry home on their heads for the fire. Later the little girls had a tiny pot put on their head, perched on a miniature grass carrying-ring and went to the water-hole with their nurse girl to fill it and carry it home without spilling the water.

Young Ngoni children among their siblings and age-mates

The hard-worked theme of sibling rivalry among small children in a family was not obvious among young Ngoni children. I expected to see outbursts of jealousy when the ex-baby returned after weaning to his mother's compound and found another baby installed there. But even with the new baby present, the mother seemed to have time to pet the ex-baby, telling the nurse girl to leave him with her, and there were few overt signs of emotional tension. This was certainly due to a large extent to the nurse-girl pattern, the fenced compound which was the child's home, and the interest of older sisters in their younger brothers and sisters. Young children growing up, as we have seen, were the focus of attention for a group of girls and women of different ages. They were hardly ever in a situation in which they had to struggle to assert themselves against a sibling, or, in their early years, against their age-mates. If they felt slighted or miserable or hungry or tired they could always go to someone to be petted or fed.

Hence their emotional needs for affection and attention never seemed to be unsatisfied. They were accustomed to having their physical needs supplied by any one of several women, and did not depend only on their mother for these needs. Nurse girls and older sisters were often demonstrative to small children, and they got more actual petting from them than from their mother or grandmother. Young children in turn often petted one smaller than themselves, or a new baby, and there was a contented affectionate relationship between children in the home which indicated the absence of any acute sibling rivalry.

From about the age of five or six, boys, who were escaping from the restrictions and security of the compound to the freedom and competition of village life, found a new challenge in a large group of their own age-mates, also just coming out of the younger child seclusion of the home. Boys

86

of this age, escaping from the women, showed their independence in their choice of games and occupations, many of
which, as we have seen, were of an individual nature. They
were not much inclined to join together as an age-group
except for occasional gang enterprises. If one boy interfered
with another's game of tops or took away his axe or hoop,
there was an immediate short sharp fight. The defeated one
either ran home to be comforted, with the jeers of the victor
in his ears, or he stood and sulked for a moment, and then
went on with his pursuit. It was outside in the open village
spaces and not behind the fences of the compounds that
small boys learned to put up with each other, to meet aggression and to be aggresive in turn, and then suddenly to gang
up with a group and play happily together.

The test for boys of correct Ngoni training in the childhood
stage, between weaning and second teeth, was their ability
to get on with their age-mates and fellow villagers when they
went to live in the dormitory. One boy went to live for long
periods with his maternal grandmother in his mother's home
village, after an argument in which for once his father was
overruled by his wife and her family. This boy was indulged
and spoiled by his maternal relatives who were afraid to
correct him and to discipline him because he was the child
of their son-in-law. The result was that when the boy came
back about the age of seven, on his father's insisting that he
should take part in herding and live in the dormitory, he
was selfish, rude and disobedient, and failed to fit in with
the other boys. This and similar stories were often quoted to
show the importance of the father's family being in sole control during the early stages of childhood.

V

Village Life for older Brothers and Sisters

Second teeth : a new stage

We saw in Chapter II that Ngoni children who lost their first teeth, and acquired their second, had reached a new stage in their development. The obvious gaps in their mouths were filled, and this might happen between the ages of six-and-a-half and seven-and-a-half, and some of the children might be rather small and slight for their age. Socially, because they had their second teeth, and because it was a sign of physical change recognized by everyone, the Ngoni adult would regard these children as ready for a different kind of life than that described in the previous chapter. The children were no longer dependent on adults for the detailed care and attention which we saw in the last chapter spelled security for the young child because every need of his was met. These older children could feed themselves, wash themselves, say what they wanted, speak correctly; and were beginning to behave as Ngoni children were expected to behave in all the relationships and activities of daily living. They were still in the wider sense dependent on adults for their basic needs—food to eat, a place to sleep in, tasks to perform, care when sick. But they had passed completely out of the hands of nurse girls, and the boys, to a very large extent, out of the control and surveillance of the women.

A new-found independence had begun to show in the little boys before they got their second teeth. Independence then meant running out of the compound to the freedom of the village. At that time young children might behave outrageously and be punished for it, but they were not held accountable. The nurse girls and the mother, or some other adult, was blamed for letting the child grow up with such an uncontrolled temper or appetite or tongue. Once children were recognized as having passed the young child stage, that is when they had their second teeth, they themselves were held accountable for their behaviour and punished more severely, even though parents were also blamed for careless upbringing. The social sanctions of rebuke and ridicule, which began to operate in the later years of young childhood to only a limited extent, were now seen in their full force, made use of by adults, and still more effectively by the children's own age-mates. The fear of estrangement, of social ostracism as the penalty for failing to conform to the required manners and ways of living, had increasing force as the children grew older. As little children they were buttressed and protected by adults in their childish quarrels with, and moods and attitudes towards, other children. As boys in the dormitory and as girls in the girls' circle they had no longer such protection, and the result was that they became increasingly sensitive to the opinion of their peers. Professor Wilson in her study of Nyakusa age-villages, has called this social awareness the quality known as 'being good company'—getting on well with their contemporaries.

It was at this stage, at the beginning of the children's newly-found independence, that the ear-piercing ceremony took place. In contrast with the neighbouring peoples, the Ngoni had no facial or body markings, and it was the pierced ears which showed they were true Ngoni. In the days of warfare, captives, especially boys and men, were forcibly made to have their ears pierced, and hence a number of men in the Ngoni kingdoms who were not of Ngoni clans were found with pierced ears. Sometimes their children went to their parents and said, 'We want to be made Ngoni now.'

Children of Ngoni families, as also these others, chose their own time to have their ears pierced, though sometimes their father or father's sister or father's mother reminded them that it was about time. It was nearly always soon after the second teeth had come, and children who delayed having it done were taunted by their fellows: 'You, are you afraid, my age-mate? See my ears already have bone in them.' This was a reference to the round plugs of bone inserted when the hole was large enough. A bit of thread was put in at first, then a small bit of grass, then a fine reed, and finally a bone plug. Ear piercing was always done in the cold weather so that the lobe of the ear would heal quickly. It was carried out by a leading woman of one of the Ngoni families, who watched the children to see how they took it. They knew it was a test of courage, and however much they were afraid it would hurt, they stood like little statues during the operation, with a face as set and expressionless as when they were being beaten.

Accountability for individual behaviour was one aspect of the responsibility which Ngoni adults now began to demand from children. Another aspect was the performance of their allotted tasks. The responsibility for cattle herding was in a sense a corporate responsibility of all the boys whose fathers owned cattle. The older herd-boys had in fact to answer for the condition of the cattle they brought back every evening to their owners. They passed on, however, a number of small duties, such as care of the calves, sheep and goats, to the younger boys, who in turn were held responsible by the older boys for performing these duties. The boys' world, centred in the dormitory, recognized grades of responsibility from which no one escaped.

Another facet of responsibility which was at a later stage remarked on often by Ngoni adults, was seen in children's choice of leisure-time occupations, according to their individual manual and intellectual and artistic capacities. They stopped playing childish games and began instead to develope their skills in making things from local materials.

All of them made their own axes, knobkerries and catapults for hunting. Some were interested in music and made shepherds' pipes, or one-stringed lyres, or hand pianos of metal strips affixed to a wooden base. They composed their own songs and airs for these instruments. Others showed ingenuity in making elaborate models of lorries and aeroplanes, or in carving heads of animals. Others liked to weave fibre into the wide-brimmed hats some herd-boys wore.

More significant still for their future social relationships, they began now to choose their own intimate friend and to form the friendship pacts which were characteristic of Ngoni society, and regarded by adults as important in the child's development. In the friendship pacts, especially those between boys, there was no implied or manifest restraint. They could have 'joking relations', and hence say outrageous things to each other. They could quarrel and make it up, and defy each other's wishes and decisions, without a final breach. The relationship between friends often lasted into later adult life, and was probably all the stronger for the occasional lapses and outbursts, and by the fact that in the daily companionship of friends the burden of observing 'respect' did not oppress them.

The boys' dormitory

The hut known as the boys' dormitory and the whole system of living which it represented was a traditional feature of Ngoni village life. In their culture it had three main purposes. Formerly, when as they said 'War was our school', it was the place where boys slept and lived together, and where they learned to defend themselves and to obey authority. It was in a sense the preparatory school for the regiment, and the herding of cattle was the basis of the curriculum. Once a boy went to sleep in a dormitory he never left it until he married, unless he was seriously ill. In the days of warfare, he learned in the dormitory and out herding the cattle, a knowledge of the bush and its wild life and of his fellows, and the qualities required in self-defence and in mutual aid which he would need when, at the age of eighteen or so, he was called up into the new regiment formed by the Paramount. Dormitory life was therefore rooted in the Ngoni past and though its original purpose and outcome had disappeared with the suppression of tribal wars, it was still part of the organization for herding cattle and was regarded as a necessary training ground for young manhood. In very large villages there was more than one dormitory, each placed in a section of the village surrounding a cattle kraal. Boys belonged to the dormitory of that section where their parents' household was situated. There were occasional attempts sponsored by certain missions to set up a separate dormitory for boys who were baptized Christians or in an inquirers' class. This kind of separation was greatly disliked by the Ngoni on the grounds that they did not want anything to divide their people. They regarded dormitory life as an important co-ordinating factor in their young peoples' development, and they did not want the tradition to be spoiled. They therefore opposed any sectionalizing of the dormitory system except on the geographical lines already mentioned, which allowed for the full operation of the two remaining purposes of the dormitory in Ngoni culture.

The first of these purposes was to remove boys, once they had their second teeth, from the influence of the women. Ngoni men were outspoken in condemning the effects of all women's influence on boys. They made a slight exception in favour of the mothers and grandmothers of high-ranking Ngoni clans. Non-Ngoni women they always suspected, and often rightly, of introducing youths and girls to ideas and practices which were contrary to Ngoni custom, particularly in connexion with sex and magic. It was partly a belief that dormitory life would 'Ngoni-ize' the boys and counteract non-Ngoni influences from whatever source that made them so unyielding about boys leaving the women's supervision at what they considered a crucial stage.

There was no doubt that this abrupt transition, like the sudden weaning, was a shock for many boys between six-and-a-half and seven-and-a-half. From having been impudent, well-fed, self-confident and spoiled youngsters among the women many of them quickly became skinny, scruffy, subdued and with a hunted expression. The subdued and hunted looks passed off as they adjusted themselves to their new environment and there were boys, generally those exceptionally well grown and physically strong, who showed no apparent signs of shock. They all, however, showed the effects of irregular and inadequate feeding. The younger boys were chronically hungry and their hair and skin and bony knees and ribs were eloquent of calory, protein and vitamin shortages.

The other main purpose of dormitory life in Ngoni culture was to mix up all the boys in the village and let the common life together teach them how to get on with their age-mates and knuckle under to their superiors in age. Age and strength were the only criteria for authority. Older brothers might try to protect and intercede for younger brothers but it was not encouraged. All the young ones had to take their chance equally, without regard for their family name or their father's position.

The dormitory was primarily a sleeping-place, but through the group of boys who slept there the herding of cattle was organized and the off-duty amusements and occupations of the older boys were planned. The young ones had to 'fag' for the rest, fetching wood and water, keeping fires going, sweeping the hut, taking messages, huddling in a corner at night when the oldest boys brought girls in, and submitting to beatings both as a warning and as a punishment. They were usually beaten once or twice soon after their arrival and then threatened with much worse if they ever divulged what went on in the dormitory. It was not however a torture house, far from it, and the boys boasted of belonging to 'our dormitory' and were proud of having their own hidden life

93

there. It was a rough Spartan existence, where individual feelings and preferences had little scope, and where the younger ones were kept busy from dawn to dusk. Ngoni elders believed and indeed it was a key concept in their culture, that boys should be kept busy all the time and made to wash in cold water. Bathing in the cold streams of the Ngoni highlands was part of dormitory life. No Edwardian father talked more piously and convincingly about the merits of cold baths than Ngoni parents did.

The boys living in the dormitory continued to be fed from their mother's household. The older boys had their food brought by a child to the kraal gate as was done for their fathers. The younger ones sometimes fetched their own and took it to the kraal gate where they sat on the extreme edge of the men's group. More often they were given what was left over from their fathers' and older brothers' servings. This procedure accounted for the inadequate amounts eaten by the younger boys, though they drank some milk when milking the herds and out at the grazing grounds they made curds and caught birds and baked them in clay. Sometimes the desperation of hunger drove them to steal maize cobs or ground nuts from their mother's granary to roast in the ashes of their fire. This kind of stealing was condemned as very wrong by Ngoni standards, and sometimes older boys, in order to show their authority, forced the young ones to steal in this way on their behalf.

What effect did dormitory life produce on the boys? The Ngoni parents, the fathers that is, expected it to produce toughness, leadership, responsibility and respect for authority. On the whole it was successful. The Spartan life ensured toughness, the herding of cattle demanded responsibility and leadership, and the smooth running of dormitory society was based on respect for authority and obedience to it. From time to time the younger boys ganged up together to protect themselves from over-exploitation, and learned in these efforts at resistance the value of joint action. There was considerable latent, and at times overt, antagonism from the younger towards the older group. This was to some extent mitigated by the dominant interest as well as occupation in cattle-herding. The head herd-boys were people of import-ance, called in for consultations with the adults who were cattle-owners. They assisted at the killing of beasts and went with them to market when beasts were sold. These older boys, despite their dominance, were heroes to the younger ones, and basked in an aura of hero-worship. They took good care to build up their claims to be thought of as 'big ones', with proven feats of strength, vaunted knowledge about cattle, skill in leading dances, and reputations as lady-killers.

The younger boys found some outlet for their aggressive impulses in the stick fighting, which was a recognized sport. They fought with 'rods', like single-sticks, and became adept at attack and defence. It was alleged that in the old days there was no redress for broken heads or bruises. As the elders said: 'They were learning to fight when young. There was no man ignorant of this learning. This school for fighting made strength in the body.' The clash of sticks could be heard out on the grazing grounds by day or in the evening on the edge of the village when the cattle were safely in the kraal. Skill in stick-fighting was one of the ways in which leader-ship among the younger boys was acknowledged. It was a kind of knock-out championship, hotly contested, until every-one agreed: 'That one—he has excelled.' Boys going to school took their sticks and knobkerries with them in case they were challenged on the path, but they were careful to hide them in the bushes just before arriving at the school.

Boys' life in the village

When the boys went to live in the dormitory they did not only escape from the women's world into a boys' circle. They entered the fringe of the men's world and provided they con-ducted themselves with propriety they could sit on the edge of the men's group at the kraal gate and listen to talk about men's affairs. The kind of topics discussed by men at the kraal gate included hunting, in the right season; cases heard in the courts and the application of Ngoni law to all subjects of the Ngoni chiefs; the organization of village affairs from tax collecting and dealing with tax evaders to beer drinks and burials and building houses; the sales of cotton, tobacco and cattle at near-by markets and the current prices; the various labour recruiters combing the villages for likely young men and the latest stories brought back by men who had returned from working in the south. Every now and then, particularly when the talk ranged round decisions in the courts or adding to the herds of cattle, references were made to the Ngoni past, to their relations with Europeans, both missionaries and officials, and to the behaviour of the non-Ngoni groups in the Ngoni kingdoms. The older boys listened attentively and as we shall see later in Chapter VII acquired among other things an extensive knowledge about the needs and uses of cattle. The younger ones pricked up their ears now and then when a familiar name or event was mentioned, and stored up questions to ask their father at a time when he was willing to listen and answer.

There was the usual Ngoni formality about where people sat at the kraal gate. The most senior men sat on each side of the opening, leaning up against the gate-posts, with the rest in decreasing order of rank as they were farther from the gate. The cleared space on each side of the gate and in front of it was all known as the 'gate of the kraal'. The craftsmen who were carving wood or twisting bark rope, making baskets or plaiting mats, sat according to their age and rank on the edges of the senior group or among them. They could have carried on their trade anywhere, but they preferred the company of their fellows and did not want to miss listening to the talk or the arrival of strangers. The herd-boys, when they were present, were on the extreme edges of those sitting there, divided into two groups, 'youths' and boys. Each group made its own fire for boiling milk and roasting sweet

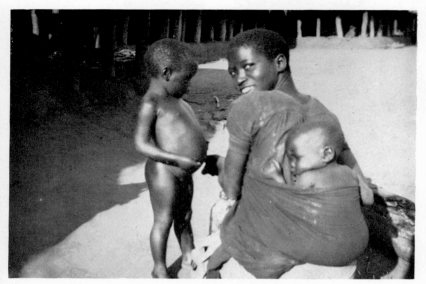

14. Mother and babies

15. Nursemaids with their charges

16. Traditional hair styles

17. Girls sitting correctly

potatoes or ground-nuts. Round their fire when dusk came on, the boys who were under fourteen asked each other riddles. The children, for girls did it in their own groups too, called riddles 'our lovely sitting game', 'our lovely wise sayings for little children', 'our wise sayings which were puzzles'. The use of riddles and their enjoyment was confined to children between about seven and fourteen, never older, and was only a game for after dark, never played in daylight. About the age of fourteen they suddenly dropped them, and if asked about them said, 'Yes, we once played at riddles, when we were young'.

Here are a few from the vast number of riddles known to the Ngoni children:

The live thing bore a dead thing and the dead thing bore a live thing—the fowl and the egg.

A large garden reaped into the hands—a man's hair.

My mother's food is sweet and cool in the morning and the evening but hot at midday—the sun.

What is it that goes on four legs in the morning, on two at midday, and on three in the evening?—a man, who crawls on hands and knees in childhood, walks erect when grown, and with the aid of a stick in his old age.

The hut of my mother has no door—an egg.

The little birds drink at one well—the roof rafters which meet at the top.

The roof is leaky—a basket-work beer-strainer.

Sitting round in a circle so that they all faced inwards towards each other, the children flung these riddles into the group, sometimes expecting anyone to reply, sometimes pointing at one child and addressing the riddle to him: 'Thou, there. Listen.' They jeered at slow and inept replies, and applauded quickness and correct answers. It was clear that riddles were partly a test of intelligence and of memory, partly a play on words with a humorous twist in question and answer, and partly a test of alertness to catch the meaning

G
97

of the riddle. An unexpected reply or a good guess often drew applause, even if it was not the accepted correct answer.

Before it was dark, all the herd-boys joined in what they called 'drill' on the flat space where they milked the cows in front of the kraal gate. As a rule this 'drill' was practising for the *ngoma* dance which took place after harvest and was the only dance for boys and girls approved by the Ngoni rulers. Sometimes they varied this dance, practising with swift follow-my-leader manoeuvres, turning, twisting, lifting sticks, knocking knobkerries together, stamping, whistling. As we have said already, the Ngoni had no drums, and all the precision and rhythm in any dances or concerted movements depended on exact timing and following the leader. The accuracy and precision reached was remarkable, and represented a high degree of intense concentration and co-operation among the dancers or 'drillers', who developed an almost intuitive knowledge of what the leader was going to do next. This dancing was practised in front of the men and older youths on purpose. They criticized it freely, and sometimes, though rarely, praised the boys. More often they came forward to show them how to do it better.

For the greater part of the day the herd-boys were with the cattle. They rose before it was light, undid the kraal gate, and as dawn broke led the cattle to the river. Then they went to the grazing grounds which according to the season were near or far from the village. As the dry season advanced and the grass became poorer, they had to go farther afield to find grazing. They returned to the village about ten o'clock and milked the cows and took the milk in gourds to the senior women, keeping some as their own perquisite. The cattle were driven under some trees to rest during the heat of the day, and taken to the grazing ground again about two and brought back about five, watered and put in the kraal and the gate was closed. Variations in this time-table depended on the seasons, the quality of the pasture, and on whether the herd-boys went to school or not.

The youngest boys were not expected to herd cattle until they were ten or eleven years old. Their work was to look after the calves, sheep and goats, sometimes following the cattle to the grazing ground, sometimes wandering round the edge of the village, avoiding the cultivated areas until after harvest. At that time cattle, calves, sheep and goats were driven into the stubble and left to forage.

As a result of dormitory life, combined with cattle-herding, a definite ideal herd-boy personality developed. This was fostered by the hero-worship of the older herd-boys by the young ones. It was also built up by the praise or blame meted out for herding well or badly by the older herd-boys to younger ones, and by the cattle-owners. This 'ideal herdsman' was used by Ngoni ministers and teachers living in the villages to relate their teaching about Christianity to the life around them. Prayers near the kraal, conducted by an Ngoni minister each evening, or before people went on a journey, often began with the words 'Jesus our shepherd, keep us well'. Young teachers often said to me how they always listened as boys when a prayer began like this, and that in school their favourite Bible story was that of David the herd-boy.

When there was a school in the village or near by which the Ngoni elders approved of, the herd-boys had a busy life. They watered the cattle very early, took them to graze and milked them. Then they went to school from ten to two, taking the cattle out grazing afterwards. In the cold weather they went to school from six to ten and herded cattle the rest of the day, after the sun had dried the dew off the grass. School attendance depended on the attitude of fathers to the new learning, and how the village elders regarded the local mission and its teachers. The boys whose fathers had no cattle, in general the non-Ngoni elements in the village, were free to attend school continuously since they had no herding responsibilities. There was some jeering among the boys in the dormitory at those who only went to school and did not go herding. School was sometimes regarded as an easy option where you sat still all day and repeated things after the teacher. This was far from being the case in a village like Enkodlweni where the headmaster was well trained and kept the boys on their toes. In such schools the boys themselves were enthusiastic about learning, and regarded going to school as a dignified and worth-while occupation, and not a childish amusement.

Girls' life in the village

When the girls had their second teeth and were acknow-ledged to have reached the new stage in their development, there was no abrupt transition for them, as for their brothers, from the household circle to the dormitory, or from the women's world to the men's world. They continued as part of the women's world; they changed their occupations and their daily routine on the whole very little; and they went on sleep ing in the hut of a widowed aunt or grandmother. All that was said however in the earlier part of the chapter about ac-countability for their behaviour was as true as for the boys.

The Ngoni girls of leading families formed a distinct group, called in the age-set terms 'children' until they were about eleven and then 'immature girls' until they reached puberty. There was in Ngoni thought and practice a clear division between immature and mature girls, and we shall see what this involved in girls' life in Chapters VI and VII. The age-set terms used to distinguish between children and immature girls did not imply any real differences in ways of living, manners and occupations. The girls between about seven and fourteen were looked on as belonging to a 'girls' circle', and this girls' circle had certain distinctive features.

In the first place the tendency of the girls to draw apart from the boys of their own age, already evident before the coming of the second teeth, was now more or less complete with the boys' withdrawal into dormitory life and their pre-occupation with herding. Later, about the age of twelve or thirteen, the girls began to take part in *ngoma* dances with the boys. This was on a village basis and organized with a view to competition with other villages. In practising such dancing, as we shall see later, the girls were often by themselves, though when getting ready for a competition they joined with the boys' group.

The Ngoni girls' circle was to some extent split into the households to which the girls belonged. There was no common residence or common eating-place for all the group, to correspond with the boys' dormitory and eating together at the kraal gate. Generally the girls continued to eat in their mothers' compound with their own younger brothers and sisters. They sometimes ate with the widowed aunt or grandmother with whom they slept, but the other practice was more common. This meant that Ngoni girls who bore the clan name of their father continued to live in the compound of their mother who might not be of a high-ranking Ngoni clan. In such cases the grandmother and the father's elder sister kept a sharp eye on the training and deportment of the girl.

The Ngoni girls' circle was an exclusive group. Unlike the dormitory where all village boys mixed up, the Ngoni girls, in virtue of bearing their father's clan name, tended to remain as a distinctive group. They were members of their father's house until they married; and when that took place it was they who could cause cattle to flow into the herd belonging to that house. It was partly for this reason, the transfer of cattle, that the Ngoni women of that house, particularly the grandmother, watched closely the bringing up of the girls from the second teeth stage onward. If she thought the training of the girl was unsatisfactory, because of the carelessness or doubtful character of the girl's own mother, the grandmother might discuss with the girl's father the advisability of arranging for the girl to be adopted into another household or into a collateral house. The reason for this was that when marriage negotiations began and the prospective parents-in-law made inquiries about the girl's character and upbringing, they would be unwilling to consider an alliance if the girl's mother were known to be a doubtful character or a careless housewife. The girl's prospects in marriage depended not only on her own reputation and character, but on the household milieu in which she was known to have grown up.

The Ngoni girls in this circle were not only an exclusive group. They were a carefully guarded and protected one. The surveillance of the grandmother, as the woman head of the girl's father's house, was dominant. Besides watching to see if the girl's home was proving a satisfactory training ground, she chose a 'companion' or 'attendant' for the girl, to take the place of the nurse girl. She was a little older than the Ngoni girl, but near enough in age to enjoy and enter into all her occupations and amusements. This companion, chosen from among the helpers in the grandmother's household, grew up with the Ngoni girl, waited on her to some extent, went everywhere with her, slept in the same hut and ate in the same household.

In her daily life in the village an Ngoni girl had in her circle all those whom she called 'sisters' and their companions. There was one exception to the exclusiveness of this group, and that was the school. Many Ngoni fathers who decided that school was a good thing for their boys, decided that it would also be wise to send their girls to school, especially if they showed signs of exceptional ability and leadership. This was sometimes carried through in the teeth of opposition from the grandmother, but the father usually won the day. For Ngoni girls school was an escape from the relative dullness and monotony of compound life, as also from the continual surveillance which became stricter as they grew older and entered the immature girls' group. The Ngoni girls enjoyed mixing with boys, being taught by men, learning to read and write, hearing Bible stories. The daughters of Ngoni chiefs and heads of leading clans were easily distinguishable in the schools by their controlled and dignified behaviour in class and in the playground. They were not given to giggling and putting their head on one side when asked questions. They took their school work seriously in order to show that they, the Ngoni girls, were the intelligent ones. They were also aware that the number of cattle to be transferred at their marriage would be greater according to whether they finished school in Standard II, III, IV, or even VI.

Apart from going to school, which was only for the daughters of relatively forward-looking Ngoni fathers, the girls continued to take part in the daily routine of the household. They and their companions, according to their growth and strength and pleasure, did a little pounding, fetching water, grinding grain, roasting ground-nuts. In a large household, where there were many helpers, the daughters of the family only did as much as they felt inclined of the domestic chores. As they said: 'It was like our play.' They spent more time with the young children, or washing themselves and their clothes by the stream. Combing and dressing their hair, rubbing fat or oil on their skin, threading beads, plaiting grass or fibres, learning how to make Ngoni bead designs for head bands or wristlets—all these formed the lighter and more amusing side of the daily routine.

From among the girls in this exclusive and protected girls' circle, Ngoni girls chose a particular friend, whom they always addressed as 'my friend', even if she were a classificatory sister or cousin. As with the boys in the dormitory this friend was a confidante to whom a girl could talk freely about her life in the compound, her likes and dislikes among the other girls and women, her ideas about suitors and marriage. The friend was always from another compound and of a leading Ngoni clan. The two friends made bracelets and necklets for each other, and went to bathe in the stream together. Sometimes the friendship lasted until the girls were married and separated. At times it broke up suddenly in a violent quarrel. There was however a curious tenacity about these friendship pacts, and they were more often maintained than dissolved. The element of secrecy in the confidence exchanged gave the girls a much-needed sense of privacy, and the freedom of being able to say anything to the friend was a relief from the constant guard on speech and manners.

The girls had dance-groups, and practised dancing in or near a compound. Each group had an 'owner' who called the others together and organized the dancing. These were several dance-groups, in contrast with the boys' single group, and the girls' groups were often rent by internal quarrels, leading to splits in the groups.

The dance-groups, and other little knots of girls, often had violent quarrels in which all their latent aggression came to the surface. They shouted at each other, scratched each other's faces and burst into tears of anger and frustration. If senior Ngoni women were around when these scenes took place, they generally broke in and rebuked the 'owner' of the group and sent them all home. Sometimes they deliberately turned their backs, leaving the girls to fight it out among themselves, or hoping the 'owner' would restore order. The senior women, rather unobtrusively as a rule, kept an eye on the girls in their dance-groups and at other times, and were adept at summing up their characters and looking out for signs of leadership and of ability to control others.

One type of leadership was often shown when a girl collected younger children together, for singing, games or for telling stories in a recitative form with a refrain in which the others joined. There was a certain kind of skill in reciting these stories, recognized alike by the children listening and by adults watching from a distance. The Ngoni believed that this skill was due to a gift for eloquence, not so far removed from the eloquence of the man who chanted the praises of the chiefs, or the man who composed his own songs. This eloquence was said to come 'from the chest'. Ngoni men and women passing a group of children spellbound at the recital of a story would say: 'Ha! look at that one. She has that which is of the chest—real eloquence.'

VI

The Threshold of Adulthood (i)

The study of adolescence

Studies of adolescents as an age-group, of the adolescent boy and girl in society, and of the characteristics of the stage called adolescence, have assumed certain principles and have stated certain conclusions in terms of western society. These theoretical leads need examining closely before they can be applied to, or assumed to have validity for, non-western societies. This points on the one hand to the problems raised in Chapter II of the emphasis on individual psychological development in western studies of childhood and adolescence. It also suggests that a follow-through of any culture-personality study, whether in homogeneous relatively isolated cultures, or in rapidly changing cultures, involves a re-examination of the relation between individual development on the one hand and social control and training on the other, and this latter requires an analysis of the aims of the society in terms of its methods in bringing up its children.

Several questions need stating here in general terms and these in turn lead to specific questions about Ngoni culture and society. Are there cultures and societies in which childhood can be said to end at a particular age or stage? Are there others in which adulthood is said to begin at the end of the childhood stage? Are there others again, as most studies of western societies assume, in which an intervening stage between childhood and adulthood is recognized which is commonly known as adolescence? If adolescence as a stage in development is recognized, what are its age-limits or other forms of limitation? And what are the chief characteristics which distinguish it from childhood on the one hand and adulthood on the other?

Studies of non-western societies suggest a variety of answers to these questions, and the answers are related to the social structure and the organization of social relations within the society, and to the economic demands made on different age-groups in the society. Societies with a marked age-set system have one set of answers; societies where economic necessity determines the role of all but small children have another. Every type of society is differently affected by the introduction of the modern school systems which cut across traditional views and practices on age-role and age-status.

There is nevertheless, as the title of this chapter is intended to convey, in every society, and particularly in non-western societies not as yet completely changed and dominated by school systems, a stage when adult behaviour and adult competence in technical skills is expected from the rising generation. This may occur before, at, or after the onset of physical maturity at puberty. A society which has exerted a conscious and directed control over the upbringing of its children regards the threshold of adulthood as the testing of its methods of socialization, calling perhaps for a re-alignment of emphases in training, in view of the advent for these young people of greater responsibility in social relations and of demands on them for effective economic co-operation. In other words, this threshold of adulthood is a test of the effectiveness of training children and young people to conform to the personality pattern of the culture of the society, and for the young individuals themselves a test of their adjustment to that pattern.

Initiation schools

The study of adolescence as a recognized stage of individual development in non-western societies has been influenced by three main factors: the attention paid to the physical changes at puberty and their subsequent implications for marriage and sexual life; the social recognition by the society of the significance of this change; and the rituals which marked this transition. Initiation rites, as a form of *rites de passage*, occur in many societies immediately after puberty. The majority of these initiation rites takes the form of a 'school', involving a period of seclusion in some remote locality away from normal social life, varying degrees of physical endurance tests, instruction in traditional hygiene and sex life and in correct behaviour to senior people, with an intense emphasis on submission to authority. At the end of the seclusion period, which varies in different societies from a few weeks to three or four months, there is generally feasting and other forms of rejoicing when the initiates return to their villages to resume normal life but with a new status.

The underlying aim in many initiation rites was to bring home to the individuals, and to the entire age-group which they represented, the dominant importance of fertility in the life of their society. This lesson among the Cewa, one of the ethnic groups living close to the Ngoni, was driven home by a second ritual which occurred at the first pregnancy of every married woman. In sociological and psychological terms the aims of the ritual in initiation schools were to strengthen the individual at a time of crisis in his life, to sanction his new status in society after the period of seclusion and instruction, and to assert the authority of society over the individual through the solemnity and rigour of the ritual. One purpose of these rituals which has not received much attention was to bring together separately boys and girls in homogeneous sex and age-groups for the last time before they broke up into separate heterogeneous relationships on marriage.

Ngoni puberty rituals

The Ngoni, unlike the ethnic groups by which they were surrounded, had no initiation schools either at or after puberty. In spite of their cultural emphasis on the importance of 'staying together', they did not make the occasion of physical maturity an opportunity for driving home the lesson. According to Ngoni tradition the forms of private ritual for girls and for boys had come with them from the south. At one point in their wanderings, said to be in Tanganyika before they settled in Nyasaland, they gave up the practice of circumcision, also brought from the south. This rite, according to tradition, had coincided with boys passing out from herding cattle and being called up into a regiment.

The question naturally arises why the Ngoni adhered to their private ritual at puberty, and never adopted any of the local forms of initation schools, and why they abandoned their only corporate ritual of this type: the circumcision school. Various reasons were given by the Ngoni elders for abandoning the circumcision ritual: that there were no more grass to be found of the sharp kind with which the foreskin was cut; that the school which lasted three to four months delayed for too long the intake of young men into the army; and that the young men of non-Ngoni families, compulsorily absorbed into the army, objected strongly to being circumcised.

After a short description of the private ritual for girls and boys, we will return to answer the question why the Ngoni held to these forms.

Girls' private ritual

When a Ngoni girl found she was menstruating for the first time, she stayed in the hut where she was sleeping and called her companion or her friend and told her what was taking place. Ngoni women declared that their girls were as a rule unprepared, and that the flow of blood was unexpected and alarming. Some Ngoni girls agreed that this was true. The majority said, 'We knew about this from our older sisters and companions, but we hid this knowledge from the elders.' The companion or friend found a senior helper in the grandmother's household, generally the one who had supervised the girl's former nurse girl and had continued to take an interest in the girl. This woman came to the hut, gave the girl a cloth to wear, told her to stay in the hut until the period was over, and instructed her companion to stay with her, bring her food, and look after her other needs. When the period was over, the companion told the senior helper who in the meantime had informed the girl's paternal grandmother, her father's sister (to whom a special message was sent to the village where she lived), and the girl's own mother. The information was always given in the phrase, 'This child has now matured.' The father's sister, who made a special visit for the purpose, came into the hut and told the girl to get up and follow her. A little procession formed, the father's sister leading, the girl immediately behind her, then the grandmother and other senior women of the father's house, the senior helper who had attended the girl, and finally the girl's mother. At the river the girl was made to take off her clothes and sit in shallow water, facing south-east, the ritual position adopted in all Ngoni crises of life and death. On the bank the women stood in silence and watched the girl splashing herself with water and trying to control her [shivering, until she was allowed to come out and given clean clothes to put on.

Back at the grandmother's hut, the women sat on the veranda, the girl in front of them, legs tucked in sideways, head bent in a respectful attitude. The father's sister led off with some matter-of-fact instructions to the girl. At subsequent periods she would not be in seclusion but she would take every care to conceal her condition from everyone. She must always wear a cloth between her legs, whether menstruating or not, and she must now consider herself separated from the children's and the immature girls' groups. She would sleep only with mature girls in a senior helper's hut, and must wash in the river only with them, and never anywhere near young children or immature girls. Later on, not on this occasion, the senior helper who had assisted her and felt responsible for her, told her how to keep her legs together if she should sleep with a boy, and warned her against full intercourse and possible pregnancy. This warning was followed up with regular examination to see if the hymen was intact, carried out every two months or so by some senior woman of the girl's father's house.

When the simple ritual was over, the grandmother sent for the girl's father and told him what had taken place. He in turn told the male members of his house and the elders of the village. The news 'So and so's daughter is now mature' was received in the village with quiet rejoicing, and the father was congratulated as one who would in time receive cattle on his daughter's marriage.

In this ritual the seclusion, washing with cold water and facing south-east in the river were the only strictly ritual acts. Equally important in Ngoni thinking however was the reassertion, at a critical time, of the authority of the women of her father's house over the girl. The girl was also made aware of her new status by being forbidden to perform certain daily functions in the presence of children and younger girls. Later we shall see how the first stages of courtship followed this event.

Boys' private ritual

The boys' ritual consisted of two distinct parts. At his first nocturnal emission the boy told one of his age-mates or his friend, who went and told one of the older boys in the dormitory. This older boy told him to go to the river very early in the morning and 'wash strongly', splashing the water all over him, and to do this after each emission. This act, called 'being beaten with water', the Ngoni believed was essential to strengthen the body and assist to control sexual impulse. There was great secrecy observed about this stage, only the boy and his friend and the older boy knowing about it. If other boys said to him 'You have now matured', he denied it vehemently.

When the boy's voice began to break, and his father or another older man noticed it, the second part of the ritual took place. The father's brother went to a senior man famed in the village as a herbalist and obtained from him several kinds of roots. These were ground and then cooked either in milk or in the cud from a goat's stomach, usually the latter, for the father liked it to be known that he killed a goat for his son. If the mixture was cooked in milk, a fowl was killed, and in either case the boy was given the meat to eat immediately after the mixture to take away the extremely bitter taste. The cooking took place on a small fire by the kraal gate in the presence of the male members of the father's house. The boy was told to dip the tips of his fingers in the mixture as it was bubbling in the pan and to lick them quickly. He was not expected to show that he found the mixture very bitter as well as hot to touch. At intervals the boy had to jump over the fire, hitting his elbows and knees with the palms of his hands. The more often he did this, the less often did he have to dip in the pan because the mixture soon dried up, but he had to continue dipping and licking till there was no liquid left. The senior men watched intently all through this performance because they believed the mixture not only helped physical growth and muscular strength but would prevent impotence. When this ritual was performed for the heir of a chief, it was followed by a war-dance in the cattle kraal and the boy had to take a second dose of medicine in the kraal surrounded by the warriors. In such a case a bull was killed instead of the customary goat, and the contents of its stomach used for mixing the medicine. The meat was eaten by the boy and his father's relatives.

As in the case of the girls, this boy's ritual was an occasion for asserting the authority of the father and his kin over the boy. For him there was however no separating off into another group after this maturing. He continued to live in the dormitory, herd cattle, and go to school as before.

The significance of Ngoni puberty ritual

We now come back to the question of why the Ngoni held to this private ritual for girls and boys at puberty. There were three main reasons. The first was that each Ngoni child belonged to his or her father's house. At this sign of physical maturity, significant for the boy or girl, and for the society, the elders of the house asserted anew their authority over them, performed a brief traditional ritual, and watched during the ritual for evidence of the Ngoni personality traits of courage and physical endurance which they expected to see in young adults. The second reason was that the change at puberty was regarded as marking only one of the stages in the development of growing boys and girls. It is true it had more significance for girls, in that it set the mature girls apart as a separate group. But it was not the prelude to immediate marriage, as the girls' initiation school was among the neighbouring Cewa people; nor was it in old days the prelude for the boys joining the army. The third reason was that the Ngoni did not regard fertility as the major dominant factor in the development of young women, as it undoubtedly was considered among the Cewa. They greatly disliked the ritual and the significance of the Cewa female initiation rites and forbade Ngoni women to have any part in them. Potency among men, on the other hand, was recognized as important both for the individual and for the social group, and impotence, particularly in leading men, was kept secret and hidden from outside knowledge as far as possible. If an Ngoni woman after marriage did not bear children, it was not considered a stigma on her, either individually or socially. The common practice of marrying one of her sisters as a 'substitute', or the very common practice of adoption was resorted to. The latter was always referred to as 'putting a child into the house of So and so'.

One of the alleged objects of initiation schools among other ethnic groups was to instruct the young initiates in correct

18.   Chiefs' wives

19.   Girls dancing *Ngoma*

20. Making lorries

21. Will the wheels work?

behaviour especially to elders, and to enforce by dramatic and sometimes brutal means a submissive attitude towards authority. That objective, as we have seen, was carried out by the Ngoni throughout their training of their children, from the earliest age upwards. They were half amused and half scandalized at the idea that young people had to be put in a camp in the bush in order to teach them how to behave.

Cultural changes in the assumption of adult roles

It is necessary to look back for a moment to the Ngoni past in order to see how changed external conditions in Nyasaland had altered the sequences and the timing of the process by which youths and young girls were recognized as adults. The stages of arriving at social maturity had been speeded up by cultural changes. In the days of warfare the senior herd-boys, from about twenty years of age, were called up at irregular intervals to form a new regiment. From this time they were known as 'young men' or 'youths', and they fought in the tribal wars for five years. In the off-season, during the rains when raids were not carried out, they were called to clear and cultivate the gardens of the Paramount and chiefs, and to help build houses and fence cattle kraals. At approximately the age of twenty-six to twenty-eight they were ordered to take the head-ring, the form of dressing the hair which formerly marked a married Ngoni man, and they were told they could marry and retire from the army. The older Ngoni declared that young men were not allowed to sleep with girls at all until they joined the army. Even then the relationship had to be initiated by the girl expressing her preference for a lover, and then sex relations were limited to partial intercourse. It was at marriage, after having been given the head-ring, that Ngoni youths were called 'men'. They moved out of the dormitory and built a hut for their wives in the area behind the huts belonging to their father's house. The cattle handed over on their marriage to the bride's family were taken from the herd belonging to that house.

The cessation of warfare, the coming of schools and of a money economy, the urge to find wage-earning work and the opportunities offered by the labour recruiters to emigrate —these were a series of events which radically altered the prospects and outlook of young men. The effect of schooling, if taken seriously, and most Ngoni fathers saw that their sons at least attended regularly, was to equip boys of sixteen or seventeen or even younger to go and get wage-earning jobs. This urge to earn money, in addition to meeting demands for taxes, was strengthened because the cattle to be handed over at marriage had now to be bought from other herds, or at least eventually replaced by purchase, instead of, as formerly, being captured in war. The young men therefore felt that earning money was essential, and finding a job was regarded as a sign of manhood in much the same way as joining a regiment had been. After warfare ceased, and taking the head-ring was given up as a mark of full manhood and mature status, there was no longer any probition on marriage until a certain age had been reached. The limiting factors in the age of marriage became economic ones instead of military and social ones. Young men whose fathers were able to provide the cattle for the marriage transfer, were able to marry from the age of about eighteen upwards, build huts for their wives, escape from living a bachelor existence in the dormitory, and then go off and find work by emigrating, if no wages which they considered adequate were to be earned in the neighbourhood. These young men then could emerge from the group known as 'youths' at any age from eighteen upwards as soon as they married. If they left the village to find work before they married, they left from and returned to the dormitory, and were still known as youths. Their emigration after marriage, usually after the wife was pregnant and they had 'put a child in the hut', presented the picture familiar in areas such as Enkodlweni of villages almost stripped of their young men, and of young wives living alone in their huts among their husband's relations. The practice of returning from work in the south about every two years or so, even if it was only for temporary residence in the village, mitigated, though only to some extent, the social disintegration and upheaval caused by the absence of so many young men.

In pre-European days, girls waited to marry for five to ten years after attaining puberty. For high-born Ngoni girls a further 'pre-marriage' ceremony and ritual took place immediately before marriage. This was after the girl and young man accepted by her as a 'lover' had been courting for some time but before any formal betrothal took place which involved the approach of the two families through intermediaries, and the discussions about the transfer of cattle. The Ngoni said that this pre-marriage rite was the equivalent for the girls of taking the head-ring for the men, because when it was held it was a public declaration that marriage was now possible for the girl, and she was acknowledged as having reached adult, that is married women's, status.

This ceremony began by the senior women of the girl's home sending for her father and saying to him: 'This child is now grown up. She is ready to be prepared to enter the state of adulthood.' One of the Ngoni names for the ceremony meant—'staying in the hut as if fasting'—a ritual practice associated with rain-making by the Paramount, and with taking 'medicines' for strengthening a new Paramount or chief on his accession. The girl, with her companion, spent two or three days in a hut, hidden behind upright mats curved so that no one could see round them. They were naked except for a long soft leather cloak worn over one shoulder and tied under the right arm. During this seclusion they had food brought to them by the senior women of the girl's house. While the girls were hidden away the village women cooked quantities of meat and brewed beer to entertain friends and relatives of the girl's father. During the feasting and drinking the senior women, with the men, danced the special dances and sang the songs associated with this ritual. Some of the songs had veiled allusions to sexual intercourse and sex organs but the majority were songs recalling historical events. Others warned young wives against jealousy and strife in polygamous households, and these again were couched in veiled language, because the Ngoni preferred allusive references to anything touching on sex life.

When the girl and her companion emerged from the hut of seclusion, they were fully dressed in a short leather skirt, cut on a circular pattern, and a long leather cloak often trimmed with a fringe of tiny brass bells or small copper beads which were heirlooms belonging to the girl's father's house. The girl who was known as the 'owner of the pre-marriage ceremony' wore strips of meat strung together like beads hanging over her chest. The fat from the kidneys (always used in Ngoni ritual) was twisted into a necklace, and the skins of cows' tails, flayed and spread out were worn hanging from the waist, one in front and one behind. At the close of the ceremonies the skins and fat used for ornament were burned by a stream and the ashes swept into the water —again a typical Ngoni ritual act.

In one sense this ritual was a form of social announcement that the girl was now ready for marriage, and the marriage negotiations and full marriage ceremony followed soon after. It was also a way of emphasizing the father's pride in his daughter, and he showed it by the lavish feasting and beer, by the standard of performance of the dances and songs and by decorating the girl with meat, fat, and skins from the cattle of his house. This was the last act he performed on behalf of his daughter, for the actual marriage ceremony took place at the bridegroom's village. It showed him as a man of substance, because only rich men and leading men could afford the outlay. It also showed the girl as a virtuous woman, for the ritual was never performed unless the girl was a virgin, and the senior women had been able, after examining her, to say to her father: 'Her cattle are full.'

This ritual was given up about the time the missions began

to establish their hold. The Ngoni elders said the missions did not like it, and alleged that they gave it up for this reason. But they held on to other rituals also not approved by the missions, and it was probably largely due to the fact that there were no longer large herds of cattle to provide lavish feasts. The songs were remembered and sung by the older women when dancing the special dances associated with the ritual, holding in their hands short rods and small rounded shields, and making stiff jerking movements of head and elbows. Such dances as were put on for me were however a relic and not a living tradition. For the Ngoni girl of good family there was no longer any intervening ritual between her private puberty ceremony and the marriage ceremony.

The marriage age of girls, like that of men, was much earlier than formerly, the most usual age being from sixteen upwards. Most of the older women held that this left very little time in which to teach girls all that they were expected to know before being married and leaving their own home and their father's village for good. This was a particular cause of anxiety to the senior women in areas where the young men emigrated soon after marriage, and where the girl had to maintain her own position and reputation among his relatives without his companionship and support.

Young adults in Ngoni society

We have just seen that cultural changes coming from the out-side radically altered the traditional pattern of development of Ngoni youths and girls. The net result of these changes was to telescope the period between physical maturity at puberty and full adult status at marriage, to squeeze the former eight to ten years of this intervening period into about two for the girls and four at most for the youths. This short-ened period of preparation for full adult life raised a number of problems for the Ngoni elders. They were aware, as was suggested in the beginning of this chapter, that the attainment of physical maturity called for some re-alignment of the emphases in training boys and girls. This was especially the case in the regulation of relations between the sexes, but new emphases were also needed in the knowledge and competence of young adults before setting up their own households. Boys and girls from this stage onwards were in fact in Ngoni culture thought of as young adults. They had passed out of childhood through the physical change at puberty, and though for a year or two that made little difference in their way of living, they were now regarded as in training for what lay ahead of them. For that training the senior members of their father's family still felt responsible and exercised control. But the emphasis in the training given was on what adults should know, how adults should behave, what adults should be able to do. For the rest of this chapter we shall follow up the new emphases in guiding and to some extent controlling relations between the sexes, and in the following chapter the emphases on cultural knowledge and on technical skills.

In the all-important sphere of heterosexual relations, there were certain social controls among the Ngoni which operated in the selection of a mate and in the form of courtship leading to marriage. Prohibited sex relations and prohibited marriages set up a pattern of avoidance between brothers and sisters, between parallel cousins, and between members of the same clan, and in former days the prohibition had extended also to the children of men of the same regiment. In selecting a mate the Ngoni preference was for someone in another village, for someone of an equal ranking or higher clan, and among Christian families for a young man or girl either already baptized or under instruction. This last preference, urged strongly by the missions and by Christian parents, was often difficult to reconcile with the preference for a high-ranking clan connexion. This was illustrated in the case of a young teacher, whose parents were Christians. He found himself being given contrary advice about choosing a wife. His father died, and his grandfather, an ex-

warrior, was responsible for advising the youth. He indicated
seven villages in which there were girls of good family whom
he might go and have a look at. He urged him not to marry
'a girl who belonged to another nation', meaning another
group, not Ngoni. He wanted him to marry one of several
girls in a collateral branch of the royal clan, for whom the
youth would have to give several head of cattle in the marriage transfer. The grandfather was quite prepared to sacrifice several of the cattle from his herd in order that the youth
might make a good marriage. The young man's mother and
his teachers in the mission wanted him to marry a Christian
girl. In the time after harvest he went visiting with his age-
mates, and saw a girl he liked the look of at a wedding dance
in another village. He was particularly attracted by this girl's
quiet and dignified behaviour, and by the fact, discovered
through a 'go-between', that she had been to school and
could read and write. The girl was at that time not a baptized Christian but under instruction. She was also not of an
Ngoni clan, but of one belonging to a neighbouring ethnic
group. He pursued his inquiries and found that her parents
had been brought up in an Ngoni village and 'knew Ngoni
customs because as children they had grown in Ngoni hands'.
He married this girl, greatly to the disappointment of his
grandfather, who felt that if the father had been alive he
might have been able to find possible choices for the boy
which would have reconciled the Ngoni ideal of marriage to
a high-ranking clan with a Christian background.

In pre-European days there had been a series of 'dynastic
marriages' between the royal clan and the leading clans and
the desire to link the aristocratic families in this way was
very strong still. It was always alleged that the girl had the
right to refuse a suitor if she did not like him. I found several
cases however in which the girl's refusal had been overruled
by the men of her father's house who desired a 'dynastic
marriage'. In two of these cases the girl was finally carried
off to her husband's village for the marriage ceremony after

a strenuous resistance, during which one of them earned the name which stuck to her ever afterwards of 'the biting spider'. Considerations in choosing a mate, both for youths and girls, were not only influenced by the Ngoni desire, especially strong among the senior people, for linking Ngoni clans and families together by marriage. The high proportion of young people, boys especially, who had been to school and were Christian, weighed the scales in favour of an educated Christian wife or husband. As always, however, the factor of personal liking was very strong. Attraction first, and then liking based on further acquaintance, was held as most important by the youths and girls themselves. It was partly the question of the transfer of cattle to seal the marriage contract which inclined the young men to listen to the advice of their elders, for they were dependent on them, at least in the first instance, for providing the cattle.

The other direction in which social control operated in relations between the sexes was in the forms of courtship tolerated and permitted. In pre-European days, and for a long time after the missions came, the age of marriage was, as we have seen, postponed for many years after puberty. In those days there was a recognized and socially accepted pattern of sexual freedom before marriage, which we have already mentioned. A girl could indicate to a young man, who had recently joined a regiment, and had shown in various ways that he was attracted by her, that she was willing to take him as a lover. Often this relationship led eventually to marriage between the two, but it was not always the case. These two slept together from time to time in the dormitory, practising limited intercourse. The fear of being deflowered and still more of being pregnant before marriage acted as a very strong deterrent to the girls not to let the young man, in the Ngoni phrase, 'harm her in any way'. If this occurred the girls knew they would have no pre-marriage rite and no full public wedding ceremony, and this would bring shame not only on them but on their father's family and house.

The missionaries, and through their influence Ngoni Christian teachers and ministers, tried to put a stop to this form of courtship. It was very difficult to convince Ngoni elders and young people that a practice which had been considered socially correct and was under some measure of social control, was now wrong and must be given up. They saw it as something quite distinct from casual and promiscuous intercourse, which they discouraged and despised. A young Christian teacher, speaking of his own youth, said: 'The Christian rule forbade boys and girls to sleep together at night and to play as our fathers played. We did not keep those rules, and we visited girls at night who wanted us, but we were careful not to harm them.' The Ngoni Christian leaders who were aware of the problems on both sides finally threw their weight into advocating much earlier marriages while supporting the carrying out of the private puberty rituals. As we have seen, marriage became usual at about sixteen for girls and from eighteen upwards for youths. This as a rule, though not invariably, ensured that the girls were virgin at marriage which was a very strict Ngoni requirement. But it brought in its train a number of other difficulties which we shall discuss in the next chapter.

VII

The Threshold of Adulthood (ii)

Knowledge and skills

Towards the end of the last chapter we said that in this following chapter we would be concerned with the knowledge and skills which young adults in Ngoni society needed before they could assume the adult role of setting up and managing a new home, and of taking part in village and national affairs. Here and there in earlier chapters there have been references to 'men's affairs' and the 'world of women', suggesting that there was a range of knowledge, of activities and of competence in those activities for which preparation and training was needed for those on the threshold of adulthood.

In talking with the Ngoni about the way in which they were handing on their traditional knowledge to the younger generations, they often distinguished between two kinds of knowledge: one a wide range of perceptions and information necessary to carry out daily and occasional activities in the household and village; and the other, a corpus of traditional lore about natural phenomena, and about their history and law. This is not altogether a valid distinction since both kinds of knowledge were traditional but it is a convenient way of approaching the two kinds of instruction given to young adults. The Ngoni were often apt to stress the importance of this second kind of knowledge because they resented the attitude of many Europeans that the Ngoni, and other African peoples, were 'ignorant' until the schools came. This touched them on a very sore point since they set great store on knowledge and wisdom in men and women, and did not understand how Europeans could draw such a sharp line and equate ignorance with the absence of a literature and written traditions. When talking about how they instructed their young people in the traditional knowledge about the natural world and their own national law and history, they pointed out that there were no set periods for this kind of teaching, but that there was a recognition that the young man, before or about the time when he himself became a father, should know what his father knew. We will begin then with some indication of the kind of matters included in this traditional store of knowledge, recognizing that reference can be made only to a small selection from it. We will go on in the second half of the chapter to the other kind of knowledge which was inseparably connected with practical and technical skills.

Ngoni traditional knowledge : the reckoning of time

The Ngoni had a system of reckoning time and a recognized calendar. This consisted of thirteen lunar months in the year, reckoned from the first appearance of each new moon, and beginning with our December as the first month. The names of the months are all related to natural events, and these as the following list shows were in five main groups : when certain wild animals had their young; the time of bitter cold and frosts; when the hawks came to catch chickens; when certain trees fruited; when the new crops were ripe and the former first fruit ceremony took place.

NGONI NAMES FOR MONTHS

1	*Impala*	Antelopes have their young
2	*Inkokoni*	Gnu have their young
3	*Impuso*	Tasting new crops
4	*Inyati*	Buffaloes have their young
5	*Indlovu*	Elephants have their young
6	*Ilize elincinyane*	Beginning of cold weather
7	*Ilize elikulu*	Great cold weather

8	*Ukholo omnsinyane*	Hawks fly and hover
9	*Ukholo omkhulu*	Hawks catch chickens
10	*Isiganyane esincinyane*	Trees begin to flower
11	*Isiganyane esikhulu*	Trees fruiting
12	*Inhlachana*	Trees fruiting
13	*Umgano*	Trees fruiting

The months were more generally grouped in two main seasons: the rains, whose name meant that the earth was 'clothed and decorated with new grass, leaves and flowers'; and the dry season, the time for moving village sites, felling trees and clearing bush for new gardens, castrating oxen. It was the true Ngoni families who knew the names for the months and the relation of months to the seasons. Among these families in every Ngoni village there were men who watched the sun's movements, and noted the hill or tall trees behind which the sun set when it reached its most southerly point. This was for them one of the signals that the rains were near. If the rains did not begin when the sun reached this point, they announced that this year the rains were delayed and the crops would probably suffer. When the *inkaku* bird began to sing, the first man who heard it went to tell his neighbours to repair their hoe handles and begin to clear the fields, for the rains and the planting season was at hand. When a large flat mushroom appeared in the woodland, it too was the herald of rain.

Not only were these months and the seasons they indicated the means of regulating work. They were also the way by which the Ngoni reckoned time. They had rods for each month and notches for the days. They took these with them on campaigns, and when returning they produced the rods, and pointing to the notches they said: 'On the sixth day of the seventh month we began fighting against X's village,' or 'We reached that river on the first day of the fifth month.' Ngoni elders were however quick to point out that they were all trained from childhood up to have excellent memories, and the notched sticks were only an *aide-mémoire*, not a necessity.

The heavens and the earth

When the Pleiades appeared just before dawn they said the Pleiades were being 'reborn' (the word used for the new moon's appearance and for the initiation of a diviner), and that in this position in the heavens they were heralds of the cold season. They knew the relative positions of Venus as an evening star and a morning star, and watched for the appearance high in the heavens of Jupiter which they knew by its size. Orion they recognized as a man with a spear, a hunter, and the Milky Way as the sands of the sky, since sand was used to denote numbers which cannot be counted.

In announcing the death of a great chief by a messenger sent from village to village, the traditional formula was: 'Listen. Do you hear? The heavens have fallen.' Hence when earthquakes were felt, it was believed that some great chief had died, and the earthquake was the trembling when his spirit left the earth for the place of the departed spirits. If it turned out to be no one of their own people, they nevertheless held to the belief that somewhere, unknown to them, a 'great one' had died and his spirit had departed at the time of the earth's trembling.

Eclipses of the sun and moon they also connected with some great event either among their own people or elsewhere, and they used the eclipse year and month to date these events. Their famous crossing of the Zambezi on their northward march, finally and irrevocably cutting off their connexions with the south, was during a solar eclipse. In teaching young adults Ngoni history they said: 'When we crossed the Zambezi it became night at noon.'

A lunar eclipse, almost total, occurred when I was in a chief's village, and all the people were called to the kraal and stood watching it. Then the chief's spokesman, his 'mouth-piece', called for silence in the phrase used for a war summons or other pregnant announcement: 'Listen. Do you hear? The chief says there is a great matter being discussed. It is not here but elsewhere. The case is very important.' Then the women took their poles and struck the tall wooden pounding mortars with resounding blows. A Ngoni elder commented to me: 'Listen. They are washing the moon from its clouds, so that it may come out of the darkness and shine again.' The event was curiously reminiscent of an eclipse during my stay in an Indian village when pots were struck 'to wash the moon'.

Reckoning of numbers

The Ngoni used tens as units in counting. They began with the right hand clenched, like the fist they raised in the traditional greeting. One by one they raised from the bent-in position the thumb and each finger in turn, and then did the same with the left hand. When they reached ten they struck one hand against the other with all the fingers extended and said '*ihlumi*' (ten), and for twenty, thirty and so on they struck their hands together the correct number of times. For one hundred they used the word '*ikulu*', but it was generally agreed that this had not been in their original counting terms, but had been brought in when the Zulu Bible came to them with the first Scottish missionaries.

Ngoni history

To a people like the Ngoni whose remembered past was one of migrations, conquests and settlement in a new country, their history was no dead verbal record but a living reminder of their past achievements, and of their cultural and political differences from the people around them in Nyasaland. There were many occasions in Ngoni village life, especially in the villages of chiefs and heads of leading clans when recitals of history took place. Frequent references were made to historical events in songs, court cases, when visiting Ngoni came, in the vernacular readers used in the Scottish Mission schools, in sermons by Ngoni ministers in the churches. Fathers gathered their children together, boys and girls, on such occasions, and said to them: 'Listen. Do you hear? This is about our people from the beginning. Remember well. Do not forget, for the Ngoni cannot forget their past.'

A young man of about twenty related to me how his father, the head of a leading clan, used to talk to him about the Ngoni past when they went on hunting trips together on Mount Choma, where Paramount Mbelwa and his Ngoni had first settled in Northern Nyasaland. In among the dry grass the father showed the boy the sites of former villages, the polished floors and the sturdy door-posts of the huts, and the stumps of the kraal fences. He heard in that historical setting the story of one of the famous secessions from the main Ngoni kingdom. 'Early one morning,' said his father, 'we woke up, we who remained, and we saw that Ciwere had gone. All the people shouted "Ciwere has separated from us. He has separated indeed. Our Paramount is poor because of his departure."'

It was largely through their own efforts that the Ngoni succeeded in teaching their history to their children in the schools. More than one Ngoni leader who had been educated by the Scottish Mission began writing the history of his own people, and in their villages I found several young men recording in writing the traditions as told them by their grandfathers. One Ngoni minister, Rev. Y. M. Cibambo, for twenty years systematically recorded and checked and compared these traditions. His books in the local vernacular were used as readers in the mission schools, and later translated into English as *My Ngoni of Nyasaland*.

Sermons in church by Ngoni ministers not only referred to historical events which were illustrated in songs or recorded in oral traditions but to the role of the famous diviners, called prophets, 'dreamers of the head', who foretold the advent and manner of arrival of the Europeans. The Ngoni Christian leaders went further than this. They used the parallel of the Jews of the Old Testament preparing the way for the Christian era to illustrate and drive home their belief that they, the Ngoni, had prepared the way for the Christian Gospel in Nyasaland. 'Were we not also a people who hated idols and images? We too tried to reach the Great God through our ancestor spirits, but we failed, until the mission came to teach us.' 'We held together the people of this land under one rule so that the missionaries could travel safely and spread the Gospel teaching.' These beliefs were stated so often that they became almost standard formula, and the incongruity of this picture with some of the warlike situations recorded by the earliest missionaries was ignored and forgotten. In the churches, where the people sat on mats, Sunday by Sunday, facing their Ngoni ministers, rising to sing, in their typical Ngoni harmonies, Christian hymns set to former Ngoni war tunes—in this setting Ngoni history was brought home, interwoven with the new teaching, to young adults who formed the majority of the congregation. For Ngoni elders it was something more than a reminder of their past. It was setting the Ngoni people in a special relationship to the European missionaries and the new learning, compensating for the passing of military power and political supremacy by establishing Ngoni cultural superiority over their neighbours. This gave some spiritual reassurance to a people in the throes of political change, and it was a lesson which lost none of its significance for the young adults who heard it.

Ngoni law

'There was one law for all the people. No one could be ignorant of the law.' These were the words, quoted in Chapter I, which the Ngoni used frequently to describe the importance of law in their culture, its role in the political unification of their own and subject peoples, and the responsibility, laid on all adults, for knowledge of the law and conformity with its demands. An incident in a court of law, which was unforgettable to an anthropologist, was a case in which a chief sat

22, 23. Herd boys

24. Learning to make five

25. Explaining how to do it

in judgement on his own son, a young man of twenty-one, for committing adultery with the wife of a man of a former slave family. The husband brought the case against the chief's son, and the chief ordered the man to speak truly and not be afraid. The case was heard amid the most deathly silence. In awarding a heavy penalty of compensation against his son, the chief spoke of the central position of law in Ngoni life, and of the fact, so sharply brought out by the case, that the law was no respecter of persons.

Young adults, boys and girls, were held personally responsible for breaches of the law which they had commited. Penalties were awarded against them as individuals, even though they often could not pay the compensation without the help of their father and his family. They were expected to become acquainted with the law in various ways. One was by conformity to accepted social codes of behaviour, instilled into them by their elders, particularly in such matters as sex relations, respect for property, avoidance of slander and of injury by violence. Another way of learning how the law operated, as well as the principles upon which the case-law was built, was by attending the courts, and listening carefully to the cross-examinations as well as to the judgements. Young people were expected also to ask their fathers, and elders generally, about points of law which they had not understood, or had confused with some of the practices of the local people. The onus was upon young adults for acquiring this knowledge of the law as well as for behaving in accordance with it. We shall see in the next chapter how the Ngoni regarded being law-abiding as one of their basic cultural traits, as well as being evidence of the individual character of a young adult.

Ngoni traditional skills

We made a distinction, albeit a rather tentative one, at the beginning of this chapter between certain kinds of traditional knowledge which we have been describing up to this point, and other kinds of knowledge which in Ngoni culture were the basis for performing certain traditional activities. This second part of the chapter I have called traditional skills, to avoid the clumsiness of constantly differentiating between knowledge, skill and activities. Again, as in the first part of the chapter, we have to be selective, and I have chosen a few out of the typical Ngoni skills taught to young adults to make them efficient producers in the village economy, able to manage and direct various units of workers, and to be 'good company' in those pursuits which were for leisure time enjoyment. The young men's traditional skills which we shall look at are the care of cattle, hunting and some of their crafts; the young women's are the care of property, the storage and use of food-stuffs and some women's crafts. At the end of the chapter we shall look at certain Ngoni 'arts', which demanded individual and corporate skill of a special nature.

Men's skills: Care of cattle

The senior herd-boys, sons of cattle-owners, carried considerable responsibilities for the herds under their care during the day. By the time they gave up herding they had learned a great deal about cattle. Understanding about what constituted good herding had been handed on to them by their seniors, and they were well aware that losing an animal, failing to find good grazing so that the beasts became thin, letting them escape into the cultivated fields—all these were signs of bad herding and they would be punished accordingly by the cattle-owners. The daily scrutiny of the herds by the owners was made the occasion for blame or commendation. Every evening the owners of the cattle stood by the kraal gate as the boys drove the animals in, and the head herd-boys reported to the owners if a cow was sick, or if a bull had been mating.

Cattle-owners, since they were anxious that any cases of illness should be promptly reported, made a point of calling the older herd-boys when they were discussing 'cattle problems' in the evening. They took them into the kraal and showed them signs of the cattle not being well from the condition of the skin, udders, hoofs and mouth. The older boys were also called to be present if medicine was given to cattle, either some specific known to the owners, or treatment given by a 'specialist' called in, who might have real skill and knowledge about sick animals or be trying his luck with secret remedies known only to himself. The herd-boys were taught to notice the condition of other cattle than the ones of which they had charge, and to report on them. These might be cattle in other villages, or cattle belonging to their father's house 'boarded out' in another kraal according to Ngoni practice. The older herd-boys went with their father and his brothers to local markets where cattle were bought and sold, and listened to arguments about their condition which could make a difference of several pounds in the price they fetched.

When it had been decided in the village to kill a beast, for eating, or for selling the meat, or for a sacrifice, it was usually a young adult who was called to spear the animal. Some young men became adept at planting the spear behind the left shoulder in such a way that the beast dropped dead at once. At times two or more stabs were necessary, but it was a matter of pride and no small skill to succeed the first time. The senior herd-boys, who had driven the animal out of the kraal after separating it from its fellows, stood close round and watched attentively, for the stab had to be both accurate and forceful. The reputation of being skilful at killing a beast, of being a 'one stab' man, was greatly desired by herd-boys. They coveted equally the reputation of being skilful at flaying the beast. With carefully sharpened knives, in a few quick deft strokes, the young men slit the skin, opened it up and began to cut up the carcase. Like assistants at a surgical operation, the senior herd-boys held the knives, lifted a limb, turned back the skin, collected the blood, removed the severed portions. On branches of fresh leaves, brought by the younger herd-boys, were piled the sections of the animal, down to the last bit of intestine, for distribution according to a fixed Ngoni pattern.

A senior man of the house owning the beast, when all was ready, 'counted' all the parts, that is he named each part, head, horns, tail, feet, joints and internal organs, and each was pointed out to him as being present. The herd-boys standing round learned the names of the organs and the sections of the animal, and heard the names and status of the men to whom the parts were assigned. The herd-boys of the family of the owner were given certain symbolic parts: an ear, an eye and the nose, for hearing, seeing and smelling; parts of an artery and of an intestine as controlling the blood flow and the waste material, and the rectum as ejecting waste; and the foot for walking steadily and fast.

Some of the meat was roasted over a fire, parts like the stomach and intestines were cleaned and boiled, some was dried slowly on a rack over a fire of green wood, and put in fibre bags for keeping. The blood was taken to the head woman of the house owning the herd. She cooked it with the fat round the kidneys till it coagulated and formed a dish, salty and meaty, much liked by the Ngoni, and rather akin to black pudding. The women also took over any spare fat and rendered it down and clarified it to use as unguents.

The young adult who had had six or seven years of herding cattle and had advanced to be a senior herd-boy, had acquired not only certain manual skills such as those just described, but also some knowledge of the anatomy of cattle, some idea of the social attitudes towards cattle and their ownership, and some idea of their economic value to the Ngoni. For certain restricted ritual purposes, a cow in calf had to be killed for sacrifice, and herd-boys saw the foetus removed when the cow was cut up. They were also often present at the birth of calves in the bush, and had to wait round to protect the cow and calf, until they were strong enough to go back to the kraal.

The intricate system of ownership of cattle, including the relation between a house and a herd, and between certain herds and the spirits of former great people, was part of a herd-boy's background knowledge. He listened at the kraal gate to the men discussing questions of ownership. When a decision was taken to kill a beast, or sell one, or to transfer one or more at a marriage, or to hand over a beast in payment of a fine, the senior boys knew which group of beasts in the kraal must be driven out to be looked over in order that a selection could be made by the man concerned.

The Ngoni classified their cattle according to age, sex, colouring, size and shape of horns, whether castrated or not, whether in calf or not. Knowledge of the extensive series of names used for these 'classes' of cattle was part of a herd-boy's A.B.C. By the time he was old enough to be told to drive certain cattle out of the kraal, designated by their class, he knew exactly which ones were meant. He could also use the cattle terminology to be precise in telling an owner about a beast which had strayed or one that had a sore hoof, or one that was giving an exceptionally good or poor flow of milk.

Herd-boys learned that cattle constituted a form of wealth, not only by the numbers a man possessed and could display, but also because they were easily realizable assets. Cattle could be sold to pay taxes, debts and court fines; and to pay men working for an Ngoni owner of cotton or tobacco gardens. They learned also that since cattle could be converted into money, the men of the house owning the cattle could use the money to buy cloth. This cloth, the property of the house, was kept and looked after by the senior women, who would lend it out temporarily to young men wishing to dress up smartly to go courting or go on a visit.

In the modern forms of Nyasaland economy it was a

natural translation for Ngoni young men to become butchers and dairymen, if they could apprentice themselves to a relative, or if their father could put up the necessary capital outlay for starting independently. This conversion of knowledge and traditional skill into a channel offering higher rewards in cash incomes found the young Ngoni adult well prepared to earn his living.

Hunting

There was an aura of manhood and of distinction about all forms of hunting among the Ngoni. They did it because they enjoyed it, and not seriously to augment their family's food supply. There were two main corporate forms of hunting: the chase, when hare and deer were hunted with dogs; and killing lions and leopards. The first was the pursuit of a Ngoni gentleman which no one wanted to miss during the right season; and the second was the act of warriors defending themselves and their cattle and villages from marauders.

Ngoni boys in their herding days acquired some of the skills needed later for hunting with the men. They made traps to catch birds from the hair of cows tails or smeared bird lime on branches. They developed great adroitness at hitting birds on the wing with knobkerries. In these pursuits, which for them were half fun, half to get bits of extra food, they were training their eye, learning to observe the habits of birds and small animals, learning to track them, and developing that combination of patience, prompt action and accuracy of aim essential to successful hunting.

Some of the Ngoni men liked to go off hunting on their own, usually those who had a gun. Fathers used to take their sons on such hunting trips, and use the opportunity to teach them how to track successfully, how to put up with hunger and thirst on long marches, how to load and fire a gun. One young man described how his father used to point out to him on such trips the birds and butterflies in the bush. On one trip his father taught him to use his muzzle-loading gun, how to carry it safely when loaded and how to aim carefully. His father, who was a noted preacher, then likened aiming in shooting to aims in life: 'There are many things in the world, and when you see them you will think that you can have them all at once. But you will fail if you have no aim and do not choose what you want to aim at.'

The 'chase', the main Ngoni form of hunting in a group, took place in the hot dry season, after the grass fires and before the first rains fell. A leading man who wanted to hunt sent messengers to neighbouring villages to announce that a hunt would be held on a certain day in such and such an area. The form of the message was the same as that for mobilization for war. The villagers turned out in companies according to their old military formations; and on the night before the hunt they slept apart from their wives, as when mobilized for a campaign. On reaching the hunting site, the slope of a hill, or the head of a valley, or a shallow depression, the important people were in the centre, the ordinary men around them and the youths on the wing. All could come to the hunt, masters and servants alike.

Etiquette was strict about the kill. The first man who wounded the game with his spear called out his name, the second who inflicted a wound did the same, and so did the man who dealt the final blow. All those three were entitled to some part of the animal according to his share in the killing, and part was set aside for the 'owner' of the hunt. Spears were used in this kind of hunt, and those who had no spears, chiefly the non-Ngoni servants and lesser villagers, used long hunting-knives and knobkerries. No guns were taken on this kind of chase, but dogs accompanied the huntsmen. These dogs were trained for hunting and tracking game, and were lean and fierce but under control by their owners. Accompanying the main body of huntsmen were skilled trackers who knew the area well and could guide the hunt, calling out at intervals one of the Ngoni war-cries: 'Listen. Do you hear me? I say the game is over there.'

After the hunt the tally of kills was reckoned up, the game was carried home by the young men, and on the return to the villages the meat was cooked and eaten by the men at the kraal gate. This was the occasion for going over all the episodes of the chase, the skill of So-and-so, the fine organizing of the hunt by its 'owner'. No one mentioned the misses, no one's feelings were hurt, and there was a warm feeling of united and contented sharing in a good day's sport.

Lion-hunting was organized differently. Only former warriors and well-known huntsmen were called, and they sometimes took their sons with them as carriers. Guns as well as spears were taken, though the Ngoni liked to say, and it was often true, that they killed lions with spears only. Tracking a lion was dangerous and difficult, and when it was located in a patch of tall grass or reeds, the huntsmen made a circle round it, ready to attack when it broke cover. As in the chase, the one who stabbed the lion first, second and finally was noted. The dead lion was hoisted on poles slung from the shoulders of young men, and carried to the village where the hunt was organized. Here the party was welcomed and given food, the heroes were acclaimed, and the headman and seniors led the way to the village of the clan head, who called his men together to rejoice. When the augmented party reached the chief's or Paramount's village, where all lions had to be taken, a war-dance took place in the kraal, as of warriors returning from a campaign. The killer of the lion came out in front of the rest and danced his individual war-dance; he was hailed as a hero and new epithets were added to his praise names. The whole party was given beer, a beast was killed for a meat feast, and then the party thanked the Paramount in traditional fashion and went home.

It was in lion-hunting that young adults who were taken along felt the spice of danger, the thrill of success, and witnessed the pride of recognition for the successful killer by

the Paramount and all the Ngoni leaders. Part of their excitement was expressed by the youths in whistling, an accom-
plishment much esteemed by the Ngoni. Herd-boys learned
to whistle in one fashion in imitation of birds to lure them to
the traps. They whistled in another way to make the cattle
move faster to and from the grazing grounds, and in a more
provocative way to stir up the bulls to fight. They whistled
signals to each other over long distances across the valleys,
and they practised whistling at all kinds of times 'to make the
tongue more nimble'. By the time they were young men they
were skilled whistlers, ready to perform as an accompani-
ment to the individual dancers celebrating a lion kill, or to
the team of youths and girls in the *ngoma* dance.

Other skills

After the wealth to be earned from cattle, the excitement of
the chase and the fame acquired by lion-hunts, most other
pursuits seemed tame to young Ngoni men, especially those
related to cultivation. They got some fun however out of the
occasional communal hoeing-parties for clearing new land,
or terracing land already cleared. A gang of young men
would challenge another to do an appointed task in a given
time. The two parties would fall to, hoeing in a line, shouting
encouragement to each other and insults to their rivals such
as: 'You! You are just women. See how you hoe with your
arms bent'—with bursts of whistling and singing to keep up
the tempo of work.

The same gang spirit, calling for swift co-ordination and
good humour, showed in the role played by young men
when a hut was being built. Their part was to dig a wide
shallow pit, break up the clods of earth, and pour in water
carried to them by the women. Then they trampled the mud
until it was mixed ready for the women to plaster on the
walls. As they trampled they sang and whistled and stamped
with the high knee-bending movement of the *ngoma* dance,
emerging finally red-brown from toe to thigh, laughing at

having finished their task, and going off to wash in the river with more whistling and singing.

Specialized crafts

Ngoni elders said that in old days there were no specialists in the villages, except the iron workers who were mostly captured people, and that all men knew how to work in leather, wood, and fibres. By the time schools had been established and a variety of careers lay open to boys, it was rare to find ex-schoolboys taking up village crafts with a view to making a cash income from them. A few did, however, and their choice of a craft was attributed either to wishing to work with a relative, or to an inborn skill and liking for the craft. Tanning skins was one such craft, scraping them, rubbing in ashes and stretching them on frames. Cutting shields from skins and interlacing the front with different coloured skins was considered a highly skilled job. Making wooden spoons, wooden meat dishes, headrests for pillows, hafts for spears and knives, and sheaths for knives, was carried on in most Ngoni villages by two or three specialists using small sharp axes. They were assisted by a youth or two who liked the work, showed some aptitude for it and enjoyed sitting by the kraal gate, intent on their job, but missing nothing of what was going on. In remote villages many men made mats and baskets for household use and for sale and paid their taxes from such sales. Every man knew how to make bark rope for binding loads, fastening the grass on roofs, tying up beasts.

Musical instruments were another specialized craft, inseparable from being a musician and knowing how to perform on them. Small hand pianos of strips of metal on a wooden base, single stringed and several stringed lyres strung over a hollow gourd—these were solo instruments to accompany songs. A boy might all of a sudden decide to make such an instrument and learn how to play it by assiduous practice.

Women's skills : Guardianship of property

Ngoni social organization, as we saw in Chapter I, placed the guardianship of all wealth except cattle in the hands of the women who were heads of houses. As a Ngoni girl grew towards adulthood and the time drew nearer when she would marry and leave her home for a strange village, the leading women of her father's house initiated her into the skills needed to create and preserve the forms of property for which she would some day be responsible.

First among these skills came the care of the hut and compound. The framework and roof of the huts were built by men, but the walls were mudded and the floors of the hut and veranda were strengthened and polished by women. Ngoni women of good family did not often do the actual plastering of mud upon the wooden framework of the hut. It was considered too dirty and exhausting a job for them to do, but they had to know how it should be done, and what standards of good work involved, in order that they might later instruct others. During a hut building Ngoni girls might be seen tucking up their clothes and rather half-heartedly slapping mud on the walls, to the good-humoured jesting of the village women who were vigorous and expert at the job. The girl's grandmother stood by and said at intervals : 'That is too thick; it will fall off. Fill up those cracks. Smooth over those joins,' and so on. The girls shrugged their shoulders and obeyed while Grandmother was watching, but gave up as soon as she went away.

The flat-ended flails with which the floor was beaten were heavy and girls were generally unable to use them expertly, but they were made to watch the process, with its seemingly endless beating of the earth floor compounded of river mud, ant-hill clay and cowdung. Once the floor was beaten so that it was level and all cracks had disappeared, the Ngoni girls were made to get down on their knees and learn how to polish it with damp ashes and a smear of cowdung, rubbed in with a smooth round stone. This too was hard work, but every now and then the grandmother, watching and supervising, handed out a lump of clarified fat which quickly brought up a fine polish. The girls were told that this high polish was necessary so that people might sit with pleasure on the floor, and so that all dust and refuse showed up clearly in the morning sweeping of the hut. The floor of the veranda was similarly polished, and, as we saw in Chapter IV, the more important huts had a smeared and polished space all round the front.

In arranging the inside of the hut girls were taught the right places to put the water-jars and other pots, the baskets and mats, and the bundles of cloth and ornaments belonging to the 'house' wrapped in mats or packed neatly in wooden or tin chests. Brass and bead ornaments, and special cloths for use by men and women on ceremonial occasions, were all kept in the huts of leading women. The ornaments worn by such a woman during her lifetime were returned to the 'house' after her death and looked after in the hut of her successor. These possessions and heirlooms were periodically brought out into the sun, and shaken and aired or polished. A housewife was publicly shamed if she did not take care of such property, and people spread stories that she was careless about keeping the wealth of the house in good repair. Girls were reminded of this when they were called to help at such a 'spring cleaning', and told as a warning: 'So-and-so in that village over there, she let the insects eat the cloth of the house. The mildew spoiled the bead-bands and waistcoats. The green rust came on the brass wire. She was shamed when men spoke about it.'

Part of the property of each household was the food stored after harvest or gathered from the bush. Formerly the Ngoni stored their staple cereal in pits dug in the kraal, mudded and fired and covered with a flat rock. The same kind of pit was sometimes made in the side veranda for storing sweet potatoes, but nothing was stored in the kraal.

Maize, the Ngoni staple cereal which had replaced the tall millet they had formerly preferred, was stored on the cob in the grain stores which were described in Chapter IV. Women whose husbands could afford to hire labour to work in their fields often had three or four large grain stores, and their presence in the compound conferred importance on their owners. Inside the hut were earthenware jars of beans, cowpeas, bulrush millet, clarified fat and butter, dried chillies, while from the rafters hung bunches of herbs and dried green spinach. Some of the jars were polished a shining black, others had a blue or green glaze on them. It was a Ngoni girl's ambition to go to her new home when married with a good array of storage pots, baskets, mats, spoons, stirring sticks, and a wooden meat-dish. This would show her in-laws that she was industrious and intended to have a high standard of household management in her new home.

Varieties of food and their preparation

Ngoni women prided themselves on feeding their households well, both in variety, quantity and quality. Although they could rely on helpers to work in the gardens and to do some of the preparing of food before cooking, they always managed their own supplies and provided a variety of menus, and showed that they could cook well themselves and instruct others.

Ngoni girls clustered round the fire when a special dish was being prepared. They watched every movement of their mother as she lifted one pot off the fire and put another on, measured out water in a spoon to add to the sauce, stirred the maize porridge strongly and evenly to get rid of lumps and bubbles, washed each stirring stick in a pot of water before using it again.

There was variety in the dishes served from day to day in big Ngoni households, usually in the form of a main dish of cereal with side dishes of broth and vegetables and less often of meat or chicken. The main dish was served in the round covered food basket, the side dishes in small covered earthenware bowls. Among the traditional Ngoni dishes learned by girls were the following:

Gruel made of cow's milk and maize flour (for young children).
Whole maize boiled with beans and round peas.
Sweet potatoes boiled, peeled and mashed with tomatoes.
Beans and finger millet flour cooked separately and then stirred together.
Pumpkins cooked with ground-nut paste.
Ground-nut flour cooked with scraps of meat.
Whole tall millet pounded with ground-nuts.
Pot-roast chicken with tomatoes, onions and ground-nuts.

In Ngoni households meat when cooked in large quantities, not just as broth made from bones and titbits, was served on a special wooden meat-dish, round or oblong with rounded ends, and supported on three sturdy legs. This meat-dish was an integral part of the equipment of every 'true Ngoni' household, and, like the French housewife's omelet pan, was after use wiped clean and polished with clarified fat. The outside of these meat-dishes was often decorated with 'poker work' designs by the maker, and such decorated and shining meat-dishes were treasured as heirlooms. Other, but rare, heirlooms were hammered brass pots with a flat bottom and turned over edge, of the pattern known in India as *dekchies*. The Ngoni women who owned them declared they had been brought by their ancestors from the south.

All the extra fat when a beast was killed was sent to the women of the 'house' in whose herd it was, and this fat was cooked until it was clarified, and then stored. Butter was made by shaking milk in a gourd, and it was also clarified for keeping. Formerly milk curds were made daily by the senior women and kept to mature in a jar before being eaten. Only in a few Ngoni households was this still done.

Beer was made on special occasions when the women had

been warned ahead to pound maize and make yeast of sprouting finger millet. They then embarked on a three-day cooking programme in large pots over a log fire in the compound. 'Sweet' beer with a low alcoholic content was drawn off after the first cooking, and the rest was left to simmer and ferment until it was of the correct thickness, flavour, and alcoholic strength.

Ngoni women's crafts

Formerly when the Ngoni used leather for clothing, their women took over the skins after they had been dressed, rubbed in fat and oil to make them soft, and darkened them with charcoal made of maize stalks. They then cut and sewed the circular skirts which had a number of gores. The use of cloth, bought first from the Arabs and later from European and Indian traders, entirely replaced the former leather clothing, but senior Ngoni women still had a strong preference for a heavy dark blue cloth which they thought resembled the former leather.

Two special skills were maintained by high-born Ngoni families and they carefully trained their girls in them. One was the use of beads, threaded and sewn together to form standardized geometrical patterns, many of which had particular significance as denoting a leaf, an eye, a horn of a cow. These beads of different sizes in strong colours of red, yellow, green, blue, as well as black and white, were made into headbands, wristlets, belts, collars, and the bead 'waistcoats' worn by the men in their war-dances. Each Ngoni bride expected to take to her new home at least one food basket which she had elaborately embroidered with beads in these standard designs.

The other skill to which we have referred more than once was that of beauty treatment. Ngoni women despised and disliked the local custom of facial markings and body markings. They treated their skin with clarified fat or butter, and combed their hair with long thorns or bone combs. After washing they applied the fat to their hair and combed it out, de-kinking it now and then with strips of bamboo bound tightly to the head. They scented their hair with the juice of sweet-smelling leaves, and dressed it formerly in the high chignon. As they gave that up, they took to wearing headcloths of different-coloured cloth so arranged that beadbands across the forehead could be worn. Ngoni girls needed no urging to take this beauty treatment very seriously, and before a big *ngoma* dance, gave it much time and thought.

Only the big wives and elder sisters of chiefs could wear the necklace and headpiece of leopard or lion claws. They were the distinguishing mark of an Ngoni 'princess' or 'queen'.

The art of cleanliness

I have called this section an 'art' because the Ngoni took an aesthetic pleasure in achieving and maintaining certain standards in their homes and in their persons, which were held up to young adults as being highly desirable. This emphasis on a particular kind of cleanliness, while putting up with much that was not clean in their surroundings, was only one of several inconsistencies in Ngoni culture. The appreciation of a desire for this kind of cleanliness had not necessarily any connexion with hygienic cleanliness. It was more closely associated with the Ngoni love of orderliness and scrupulous attention to detail in the appearance of persons and places. It was also connected with what they regarded as comfort and good living. The effect of mission teaching about health and sanitation, and of government courses held for chiefs to instruct them in modern welfare measures, often caused confusion among Ngoni elders. Sometimes their traditional standards of cleanliness coincided with modern hygienic standards, and sometimes they did not. In any case it was seldom that Europeans recognized that the Ngoni had any standards to begin with, and they

26. Making clay figures

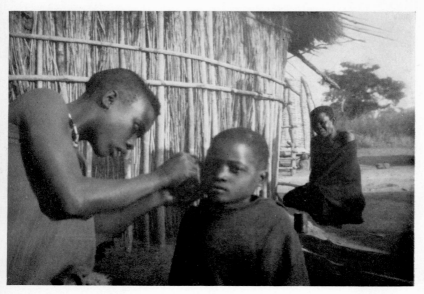

27. Ear piercing

28. Learning
to carry wood

29. Learning
to pound

generally assumed that everything was 'dirty' which was not hygienically clean. The Ngoni resented this, all the more because of their cultural insistence on decency and order, and on certain forms of external cleanliness.

Their huts, furniture and mats were often infested with ticks and bugs—neither of which the Ngoni liked, regarding them as rather disgusting. The old remedy was to leave the tick-infested site and burn the objects full of bugs. As villages became more stationary and property accumulated in the huts, and became more valuable and expensive, they built strangers' huts for visitors who might otherwise infect their own. Bugs were dealt with by bringing all bedding, mats and bedsteads out into the sun and pouring boiling water on them again and again.

Similarly it was an aesthetic disgust rather than hygiene which made them insist that there should be no spitting or nose-blowing on the floors of huts or verandas. Such actions had to take place outside, and vehement comments were made when a visitor forgot his manners in this way. An ingenious tiny iron spoon with a long handle was used by the older Ngoni for cleaning the ears and nose.

Perhaps nothing showed the Ngoni pleasure in and desire for cleanliness so clearly as the quick and apt excuses made when standards were obviously in temporary abeyance. There was no doubt that young men and girls liked looking clean and well-groomed. The daily wash in the river with soapy leaves, followed by rubbing on fat or oil made the skin glisten. We have talked already about the use of twigs as tooth-brushes, the rinsing of the mouth before and after meals, and the use of astringent fruit to make the mouth feel clean.

The same scrupulous attitude about cleanliness was seen in the washing of dishes, spoons and cooking-pots after each meal. It was almost as if the standard of housewifery was proclaimed by the sight of food baskets, gourds, spoons, etc., spread on the platform outside the hut to dry. Washing up might be a chore but when it was done in the open it was also an advertisement of high standards.

The art of speech

The Ngoni believed that as boys and girls neared adult life they should be well drilled in the art of speaking, because it was regarded as a basic Ngoni characteristic. We have seen how adults watched children tossing riddles at each other to test, among other things, their quickness of speech. Girls had been watched telling stories to see how they held their audience and showed a sense of dramatic values in recitation.

In all the standardized forms of speech such as greetings, messages, announcements, responses, young adults were expected to speak clearly and correctly, without mumbling but not too loudly. When relating an event, such as a visit, a bull-fight, or when giving evidence in the courts, they had to give an orderly account without repetition. Otherwise they were told: 'You are speaking badly. Tell it again, in order, from the beginning.' An ordered sequence of the narrative was always demanded, and, as we shall see in the next chapter, they used proverbs frequently to impress on people speaking the need to get to the point, while leaving out nothing of importance.

The art of words used with music in songs was regarded as a special gift and those who possessed it were encouraged to develop it. Inspiration for words and music was as we have seen something which came 'from the chest' and was regarded almost as if it was a special kind of breathing. Some used this gift to sing with a solo instrument such as a stringed lyre. Others used it to compose new songs for *ngoma* dances. Others again wrote Christian hymns and composed music for them, or set them to traditional Ngoni tunes.

The art of dancing

'Ngoni people think that their dances show their personality, their manhood, that which was born in them.' Phrases like this were used by Ngoni elders to try to express their feelings about their own dances, and were often said to me when we were watching youths and girls practising the *ngoma* dance, the only one allowed in the Ngoni kingdoms for Ngoni young people. On moonlight nights or in the late afternoons, young men and girls took very seriously the perfection of this art of dancing, through practising over and over again a special movement, or a section of the dance. As we have seen, they danced without drums, and all movements and changes of movement were made by a change of voice in the singing, prompted by a sudden impulse in the leader.

The competitive *ngoma* dances took place after harvest in the dry season, and were heralded by one village sending a message to another: 'The *ngoma* of the village of X will come to dance on such and such a day.' As many as fifty girls and sixty or more young men formed a village 'team', and in some dances which I saw they walked eight to ten miles to the other village, and then danced all day. Both teams wore their best clothes, with bead ornaments and headbands, coloured scarves and headcloths. The young men in the dance carried small shields and knobkerries or small axes. The girls had long rods or spears held upside down.

The visiting team danced first, and the adults of the home village were the audience and the judges, deciding, after both teams had performed, which one had 'danced most strongly'. The singing was kept up continuously, the song changing to mark a change of dance step, or a change in the relative positions of the girls' and boys' lines. The points of excellence, as judged by the spectators, were the perfect timing of girls and youths together, and the strong beating of the youths' feet on the dry dung floor of the kraal. When the verdict was announced, the leader of the defeated team went up to the leader of the victorious team and shook hands in Ngoni fashion, saying: 'Yes, we are defeated. Your *ngoma* was stronger.'

VIII
Personality and Character

Personality, culture and character

The threads of teaching and learning whose ends were grasped in Chapter II have been followed through the intervening five chapters, and our task now is to see what pattern they have made of the system of training given by the Ngoni to their children. The threads have eventually been twisted together to form two separate but linked strands, one the achievement of the Ngoni basic personality and the other the development of individual character. In this chapter I am going to use personality in the sense derived from Linton and Kluckhohn, namely the sum total of the traits which are desired by a society and form part of its culture, and which are instilled into children in the system of training set up by the society. Personality therefore since it is regarded as an aim in child training is a social product. The ideal personality is held up to the growing generation, not so much as a total achievement, but as the acquisition of a number of traits of behaviour, skills and knowledge. The Ngoni basic personality therefore consisted of common personality elements in adults, which, as Kluckhohn says, were largely a product of learning, and that learning was directed and controlled by the system of training. Character on the other hand I am going to use as the sum total of the individual's response to his training. It therefore includes his personal adjustment to the training given by the society, and, as a result, his acquiring of some or many of the basic personality traits, and hence the degree of his approximation to the ideal personality. Over and above this overt response to training, character is the distinctive individual twist given to the basic personality, together with certain special abilities and individual traits which might be in harmony with, or at variance with, the basic personality traits. When an individual showed abilities and traits which harmonized with the concept of the basic personality, he was recognized as a 'good character'. If however he developed traits which eventually showed his failure to adjust to the basic personality, then he was, or would probably become, a 'bad character'. The 'badness' was his responsibility due to a series of choices which he had made, though it might also reflect on the training given in his earlier years.

The Ngoni had a word which very nearly expressed their concept of individual character. They spoke of a person's 'own human nature' (*Ubuntu*), 'the human nature of himself'. Thus they recognized, as studies of personality and culture are bound to recognize, two distinct results of child training, arising from the interweaving of the threads of teaching and learning, namely the development of young men and women into Ngoni adults whom the society regarded as fulfilling, at least to some extent, their ideals of behaviour, skills and knowledge; and the development of young individual adults, distinguishable each from his fellows by the individual character he displayed before his elders who either approved or disapproved of him.

Anthropologists on the whole would agree with Kluckhohn that so far they have studied personality as a socially directed product rather than the unique product of each individual's growth and development. Individual reactions and responses are recognized as being primarily in the field of psychology. But the anthropologist and the educationist can make some claim to understanding this essential complement to individual personality studies. On the one hand they find the society they are studying recognizing values which do not always fit into an accepted basic personality pattern. On the other hand they become aware that individual reactions to learning, and the end product of a system of training, can never be as stereotyped and as uniform as some of the exponents of personality and culture studies would have us believe.

The outlines of the ideal Ngoni personality have really been sketched in the narrative chapters, though without stopping to point out specifically that this or that aim in training is to foster a Ngoni personality trait. I shall therefore in this chapter put together these traits, and, to introduce a new element and so avoid too much repetition, some of these traits will be associated with Ngoni proverbs. But before doing this I shall discuss those Ngoni values which I believe were the foundations for their child training.

The Ngoni system of values

The chief reason for introducing at the end of this book such an involved and difficult subject as values is to suggest that there is an inevitable connexion in any society or culture between an ideal personality and the values cherished by that society. It is therefore reasonable to follow up, and to some extent to sum up, the preceding narrative chapters of this study with a glance, for it cannot be more than that, at the fundamental beliefs and values which impelled the Ngoni people to pursue certain lines in bringing up their children. We have seen that there was a continuous and clear direction in training children which I have called a system. The more deeply one analyses the nature of Ngoni culture and the organization of Ngoni society, the clearer it becomes that there were certain definite values which they clung to as a result of their experience and of their reflection upon their past history and present and future prospects. In so far as these values were integrated into an intelligible whole, we can call them a system of values, but the recognition of such a system does not preclude the recognition also of some isolated values which do not appear to fit into an integrated system.

One of the major difficulties in examining the values of a non-literate culture is the inevitable subjective approach of the observer or anthropologist. One such observer might pursue the line suggested by the use of different persons of the verb and different pronouns in personal contacts, and the values inherent in such standardized usage. Another might choose to examine the institution of the boys' dormitory and its contribution to the total value system. Another might take the different emphases in bringing up boys and girls in relation to the fact that men were the permanent element in village society and that girls left the village on marriage. A dozen more examples could be taken from the narrative chapters of this study and usefully followed up. They would all illustrate, in the first instance, the subjective nature of the initial selection, whether the final results of several different investigations made a coherent integrated system or not. They would also illustrate the uncharted area of such studies, where there is little to guide the observer and the analyst, in spite of the growing interest in recent years in studying the value systems of non-literate societies.

Among the leads which I found most useful has been Professor Monica Wilson's *Good Company*, to which I referred in Chapter I, where she associated cultural values with the age-village system in Nyakusa society. I owe much also to help and suggestions given to me at Harvard by Professor Cora Du Bois and Dr Ethel Albert, and to Professor Kluckhohn and his associates in discussions on their published and projected series on the study of values.

The relation between Ngoni values and their ideal personality pattern is based on the study of their society and culture described in my earlier book, and on the analysis of their system of bringing up children in this book. I referred in Chapter II to certain values as group values and to others as personal values. I am not sure that the distinction is a valid one, but it is a convenient form of classification and it corresponds closely to the Ngoni way of thinking. They were continually referring to their society, or a local community in it, as if it were an integrated whole, and to the effect of individuals upon the cohesion of that society through their behaviour and actions. This was illustrated in the phrase so constantly used by them, and referred to already several times: 'He is spoiling the land,' or the converse, quoted in Chapter I: 'Young people were well taught that this behaviour was right for the upbuilding of the land.'

Among these so-called group values the first of all, and pre-eminent above all, was the value of keeping together. Taught by bitter experience that personal quarrels could lead to political secessions and to the diminution of the power and influence of the Ngoni kingdoms, the focus of much of their thinking was on maintaining cohesion whether in small units or in large. I think the Ngoni were the only people in Nyasa-land where individuals and families were not allowed to leave the villages to live elsewhere without permission of the chief or headman. In the local courts there were frequent cases in which the accused had been guilty of leaving without permission. This illustration could be used also to indicate the second of the group values. I have called it dominance for want of a better term. It involves the exercise of authority, political and legal, over their own and subject peoples, the determination to exact obedience, influenced by a feeling of paternal responsibility for all over whom authority was claimed. This was an ambivalent sentiment affecting the attitude of the ruler and his relations with the ruled, and was the basis of the court case quoted in Chapter VI, when a chief made a judgement against his own son for adultery with a poor man's wife. The third group value was that of mutual aid and trust within the in-group, in order to secure its cohesion. This was the integrating principle of the 'house' system, described briefly in Chapter I and mentioned in many other contexts. Mutual trust and aid had been in the past the main element in the behaviour of men in their own regiments, in the mutual relation of warrior with warrior, both when on campaigns and when living together in the villages.

The four personal values were inherent in the acceptance

and demonstration of the group values. The first two, physical and moral strength, and working hard and persistently at allotted tasks, were, as we have seen, instilled into children from the stage of second teeth onward. The second two, dignity and wisdom, were to a large extent values implicit in adult life, and in the case of wisdom seen specially in the contribution made by senior men and women to community life. Dignity, however, had an ambivalent meaning, as did dominance among the group values. It covered not only language, deportment, self-control, accepted rank and precedence within the hierarchy on all social occasions, but the more subtle and very typical Ngoni attitude towards 'losing face'. In the sense that young adults and even older children hated being rebuked in public because it made them lose face, it belonged to younger people as well as to older, to those called the 'humble ones' as well as to the 'great ones'.

All the emphases in child training on language, deportment, self-control, manners and inter-personal behaviour of all kinds were related to the value of human dignity, and to the concept of a person's 'human nature' as being something to be respected and built up, and carefully guarded, since it was very vulnerable.

At the end of Chapter II when some Ngoni values were mentioned, wisdom was contrasted with cleverness, and equated with knowledge, good judgement, ability to control others and keep the peace, and skill in the use of speech. The young Ngoni headmaster in the first village described in Chapter I said reflectively one evening, after listening to some of the elders talking with me about Ngoni values, 'Yes, we are different in our generation. We are proud, but they had wisdom.' It was an acknowledgement of the pretensions which his generation had begun to claim as a result of the new knowledge in the schools. It was also a recognition that the accumulated wisdom of the generations of his father and grandfather had in it an understanding of values which the younger generation had not yet acquired.

The four so-called personal values will be reflected in the Ngoni personality traits which we are going on to discuss. There are however two values which did not appear to fit into any integrated system, and which yet recurred as themes in Ngoni culture, and here and there in the ideas inherent in child training. One was the theme of childhood innocence, which was much deeper and more subtle than merely keeping children in ignorance of sexual life and intercourse. The other was the value set on the 'gentle' man. He was a man who appeared to be almost wholly self-controlled, able to have normal sexual intercourse with his wives but not always thinking about women, showing sternness but without anger, being just but also merciful. These were the qualities looked for in the man responsible for the guardianship of certain head villages where the ancestor cult was carried on, and who was entrusted with the ritual associated with the ancestor cult. In the more ancient ritual, such as carrying the sacred emblem before the armies, it was young boys, exemplifying the childhood innocence theme, who were entrusted with this charge. In the more modern contexts, many of the outstanding Ngoni ministers in the church were recognized and revered as 'gentle' men.

The Ngoni ideal personality

Chapters IV and V, as well as Chapters VI and VII, showed that there were certain elements in the Ngoni ideal of what their children should be like which were common to young men and women, to boys and girls, while others were emphasized only for girls or for boys. Among the common traits we have already seen the outstanding emphasis on 'respect' in all forms of behaviour and in all kinds of contact with older people, and with others who should be 'honoured'. Part of this respect was shown in obedience, and with this obedience in all the detailed inter-personal relations with senior people was associated, in the individual's relations to society as a whole, being law-abiding and complying with Ngoni law.

As we saw in Chapter VII ignorance of the law was no excuse for breaking the law, and the positive virtue of being law-abiding was constantly emphasized in families, villages and in the kingdom generally. Inherent in showing respect and being obedient and law-abiding was the much stressed quality of self-control. Early travellers remarked on the restrained, dignified and courteous behaviour in Ngoni villages, which was my experience also, and especially in the vicinity of leading Ngoni families. This kind of self-control was taught as we have seen in a great variety of contexts, from avoiding greedy and noisy eating as young children to putting up with being ordered about in the boys' dormitory, and from the insistence on the decorous forms of greeting and thanks to the suppression of any overt fear or pain at the puberty ceremonies.

Two other qualities were emphasized in child training since they were expected of all Ngoni people in inter-personal relations. One was generosity in sharing anything that a person had. It was a quality demanded of everyone, from the small child who was made to unclench his fist in which he was hiding three ground-nuts and give two of them to his fellows, to the big chief whose duty at a feast was to see that everyone had enough and to send food from his own portion to anyone who looked hungry. A number of proverbs called attention to the value of generosity and to the social attitude towards meanness, which was felt to be despicable. 'If you do not play with other people the grass will grow round your hut' implied that isolation and social ostracism would be the retaliation to a mean man. The reciprocal element in generosity was always implicit in the teaching and the practice and was illustrated in the proverb, often said hopefully by visitors when hospitality was not very readily forthcoming: 'I have sent my food basket to someone; the basket will return to me.'

The other quality was the conventional display of sympathy, especially at times of mourning for the dead, but also on occasions of severe loss, such as cattle dying, or illness or accident. These visits and expressions of sympathy could not be omitted without grave social disapproval. If a young man or woman was absent from the village at the time of death or loss, their first duty on returning was to go and express sympathy with the sufferer. To assist in these condolences so that the speaker and the hearer would readily understand each other, proverbs were used such as: 'If the pot is broken it is broken indeed,' and, 'When water is poured out it cannot be gathered up.' The Ngoni disliked the noisy and unrestrained forms of mourning which they saw among the people round them. To them the quiet visit and the note of resignation in the proverbs used fully conveyed the sympathy they wished to express.

All through the later stages of training children and young adults the importance of speaking well was emphasized. This at first referred to correct language and being audible but not noisy. Later, as we saw in Chapter VII, the art of speech was held up as a Ngoni characteristic, and many proverbs brought this out in ordinary conversation as well as on more formal occasions such as giving evidence in the courts. When a group of people, generally women, kept up a continuous meaningless chatter, onlookers, generally men, shrugged their shoulders and said, 'They are preparing meat without salt.' When a person talked on and on about a matter which was being discussed without getting to the point, impatient listeners, or the councillor in the law courts said: 'Your wisdom is like mushrooms which come after the cooking is finished,' or, more scathingly, 'You are the feet of a centipede' which wander aimlessly with many steps but no direction. Proverbs were not always a form of rebuke; they could also be a commendation. When a person brought out clearly the point of an argument the listeners said, 'You have rung a little bell'; and when after a prolonged discussion or the hearing of a case in the courts the audience accepted a decision as conclusive and just, they said, 'The upper and the lower teeth meet together.'

When the Ngoni talked about the separate ideal personalities of men and women, they emphasized the training needed for younger men, and to some extent also for younger women. Senior men and women were expected to possess special qualities due to their age and status and experience. It was recognized that the limited responsibilities of young men before marriage gave them little authority in village and family affairs. Since each family however was bringing up its girls to leave them on marriage and to take the good name of the family elsewhere, there was less distinction made between the qualities desired in younger married women and older ones than there was between the two groups of men.

The ideal personality of Ngoni women

This had four main aspects: physical capacity and appearance, relationship to her husband and his relatives, competence in household management, and general reputation for justice and wisdom.

We talked in Chapter III about the connexion in Ngoni thinking between women being healthy and strong and being able to bear healthy children. In the marriage negotiations and even at the final ceremony itself in the bridegroom's village, there were formalized standard questions put by the bridegroom's representatives about the health of the girl and her family, and these were replied to also in conventional phrases. Such inquiries about health had been made secretly long before the final ceremony, and indeed before any formal approaches had been made which led to the betrothal. But the fact that they were made in public on two distinct occasions, at the preliminary visit of the man's representatives and at the marriage itself, underlined the importance of health and its relation to child-bearing capacity in the ideal Ngoni woman.

We saw in the last chapter that physical strength for continuous hard manual work in the household and in the gardens was not required of most Ngoni women, though they were expected to know by experience how to hoe and to pound, to mud walls and to clean a house in order to supervise their helpers and to see that household work was done efficiently.

In addition to being healthy, the ideal Ngoni woman was always well-groomed. She might lack the facial formation of high cheek-bones, narrow nose and deep-set eyes and the light bronze colouring which were the accepted standards of beauty. Even without these natural, usually inherited, advantages she spent, as we have seen, much time every day taking care of her skin and hair. When she was receiving visitors or sitting outside her hut, her two long cloths, one fastened under the armpits and the other over one shoulder and knotted on the chest, were carefully draped and arranged. If she walked to another compound or out of the village on the road, or walked or danced in any ceremony, her dignity of bearing and poise of head was always marked. She did not hurry, but, as the Ngoni said, 'she walked strongly'. A government official passing an octogenarian Ngoni princess on the road stopped and offered her a lift in his car. She looked him up and down and said: 'Thank you, young man. I can still walk.'

Many references have been made already to the relationship between a wife and her husband, and between a wife, especially a young one, and her husband's relatives. The keynotes of this relationship were devotion to her husband, respect for his relatives, and circumspection in her relations with her co-wives and with her non-Ngoni helpers. Jealousy between co-wives was recognized by the Ngoni but not condoned, and the young wife at marriage was warned by her own family against quarrelling with anyone, co-wives, helpers or in-laws, though the last was almost unthinkable.

Competence in household management, being a successful 'châtelaine', made many demands on a Ngoni woman if she were to live up to what was considered an ideal housewife. We have talked in Chapters IV and VII of her duties in organizing food supplies, supervising cooking, and that supreme test of competence : dividing out the food so that all had a fair share. The same high standard of skill was expected in the general care and supervision of the compound, the children and the household staff. Ngoni women, like their menfolk, were proud of being able to supervise other people and organize life around them, to control others satisfactorily, to hear complaints and to pacify quarrels. The proverb 'The tooth laughs to no purpose', meaning that angry people show their teeth but with no merriment, was often heard when Ngoni women intervened to stop two quarrelling girls or to prevent an irate helper getting angry with the nurse girls.

The traits of justice and wisdom were important elements in the foundation of a Ngoni married woman's reputation. These were judged by her ability to allocate fair shares of food to servants and helpers, and to adjudicate wisely in women's disputes. Two proverbs referred particularly to dividing out food and were said about women who were either careless or stingy, and did not give their helpers a fair share. 'The finger-nails are surfeited' meant that the important people had eaten heartily without thought for others; and 'She has sliced one side only' had the same connotation, that those who had the supplies were keeping too much for themselves. Two other proverbs drove home this principle of *noblesse oblige* when emphasizing the responsibilities of married women: 'The elephant is not made heavy by its trunk,' and 'If the cows do not produce milk the herdsman is responsible.'

The ideal personality of Ngoni men

As we have just said, there was a definite personality pattern for young men whether married or not, which emphasized special qualities looked for in them, since on the whole they had relatively little authority or responsibility in village affairs. Boys and young men were expected to be physically strong, and tough in the sense of being able to do hard tasks, walk long distances, dance for hours on end, and put up with hardships without grumbling. The senior men, as we saw earlier in this chapter hated to see idleness and set great store by young men working hard and persistently at any tasks undertaken. Several proverbs illustrated this quality and were used with effect when boys were found hanging round in the village doing nothing: 'Loitering eats the owner,' 'Laziness is eating dung,' 'The garden will not be tilled if you stop hoeing it.'

Other qualities desired in young men were all connected with the values of staying together as a family and as a village group, and of fostering mutual aid and trust within the groups of males in the dormitory and in the 'house'. It was believed that they ought to be acutely sensitive to the opinion of their contemporaries, a lesson which they learned from early days in the dormitory. To an insensitive person, showing intolerance and hard-heartedness they said: 'Were you made with dog's bones?' for dogs' bones were thought to be hard and unfeeling; or, 'You have a heart like a crocodile.' A fear of social ostracism was fostered all the time and expressed in the proverb: 'The bird eats in his own field.'

There were innumerable proverbs about willingness to co-operate in all the necessary tasks which fell to the young men, such as communal hoeing described in Chapter VII, or digging the grave at a funeral. 'The eyes for seeing,' 'One arm cannot crush a louse,' 'A river grows by its little streams,' 'The heifer grows by giving it more food'—these and many others were used to admonish those who held back and to encourage those who joined in willingly. Other proverbs warned against promises of help which were not kept. 'You will eat those of the axe but not those of the hoe' was said to someone who had counted on noisy assertions of forthcoming help, like the sounds made by the chopping of an axe, and not in quiet persistent help, like the smooth almost silent action of the hoe. 'They are our kin according to their eyes' was said as a reminder of misplaced trust in those who appeared to be helpful but were not really.

Readiness to take advice both from their age-mates and from older men was another quality held to be desirable in young men. Proverbs illustrating this were: 'He that refuses instruction will be surprised by blood,' and 'He remembers that he fell; he forgot that he was hurt.' As often with proverbs, there were others with a contrary emphasis which were sometimes used as a retort to the former ones, or in self-defence. 'The inheritance was eaten by those worthy of it' was intended as a rejoinder not to interfere in other people's affairs, when unwanted advice was offered. 'The body is felt by its owner' was sometimes said to encourage a man to stick to his own opinion. On the other hand a too abrupt rejoinder, especially to an older person, was regarded as discourteous, and onlookers said 'You cause the spittle to be dry' to express extreme disapproval.

Ngoni personality in a changing culture

The direction of the training of boys had been formerly to-wards military life, and towards the qualities which made effective fighting men, and emphasized loyalty to leaders and camaraderie in the regiments. This emphasis on military preparedness was however never the sole emphasis in Ngoni training, and hence when warfare came to an end, there remained traditional spheres of influence and activity which were an integral part of life in the Ngoni kingdoms, as well as new spheres of activity opened up by missions, the admini-stration, the trading companies and the labour recruiters.

The traditional forms of activity were found in Ngoni local government which included the chief's administration and the courts of law; family and village affairs including the building up of herds and buying and selling cattle; and ritual life. The new kinds of activity included occupations such as teacher, minister, clerk, store assistant, houseboy, foreman in charge of gangs of workers. All this last group involved the earning, spending and sharing of money incomes, but even more important in Ngoni eyes, they offered opportunities of exercising authority, and of controlling and directing others.

In local government and in the courts, which formed an integral part of it, the qualities demanded were wisdom, ability to make decisions, expert knowledge of the law, skill in conducting cases and in summing up evidence, and knowledge of the people, so that their reactions to new measures and to difficult court decisions could be forecast. Certain women were thought of as inheriting this kind of judicial ability and were often turned to in private by their husbands, sons or brothers and asked to declare themselves in support of or against an important decision and to discuss its merits or demerits.

In choosing a successor to a chief the regents who were responsible for the selection looked for particular qualities of individual character as well as for evidence of the ideal Ngoni personality traits. Men who by right of inheritance could have succeeded their father were sometimes passed over because they showed characteristics which would make them a bad chief. This was one of the reasons why sons of leading men were watched so closely and corrected so sharply by the elders of a village who were noting their adjustment to the basic personality pattern as well as their individual character.

There were certain acknowledged ritual activities which demanded of the performer both a high degree of conformity to Ngoni personality patterns and special individual characteristics. On the death of a chief one of his sons or brothers was designated to become head of the 'elder' village which remained behind, when the new chief with some of the members of his father's 'house' moved out to found a new village. The 'one who stayed behind' as he was called was expected to be the epitome of all Ngoni qualities, and to have a good memory for, and an understanding of, Ngoni tradition. In all the selection of individuals to 'enter the place' of an important person who had died, the new holder of the place had to measure up to Ngoni personality standards and be acknowledged as a 'good character'.

The new kinds of occupation open to Ngoni men as a result of education in the mission schools were of two main types: those where the holders of the job still lived in the Ngoni kingdom and carried on their work in the setting of a Ngoni village; and those which involved leaving the village and living and working outside Ngoniland, more or less out of sight and out of control of Ngoni elders.

Some of the mission teachers, ministers, and evangelists returned to live in Ngoni villages after they had completed their training, though others of course were posted elsewhere. In one of the villages described in Chapter I there had been in the early days of mission work fierce and continuous opposition to the opening of schools, as well as to the preaching of Christianity. I mentioned the old evangelist who had been threatened with death by the chief when he first took up his work. If he had left under those threats he would have lost out for ever among his people, for he would have been called a coward. He stayed, cultivated his land, grew his own food, was a great hunter, was respectful to the chief and elders, brought up his children to respect Ngoni traditions. He gradually gained the reputation of being brave, a 'gentle' man, a powerful and fluent speaker in the church on Sundays, a man of wisdom and judgement, and he was constantly asked for his opinion on village affairs. Most of the village, Christian and non-Christian alike, went to the church service on Sundays, sang the Ngoni hymns, listened to his sermons in the Ngoni language, sprinkled with Ngoni proverbs and illustrated by episodes from Ngoni life and history. Very few people in that village over twenty-five years old were Christians, but the leading Ngoni families allowed him to baptize younger and older children and to instruct them in Sunday-school. The Ngoni elders contributed to the church funds in cash or in kind, and helped to build the church and school.

The younger headmaster of the school had never been threatened with death. He came in on the tide of recognition and respect accorded to the character and behaviour of the evangelist. His grandfather, like the evangelist's father, had been a well-known warrior with his own praise song celebrating his exploits. When the chief saw the exemplary behaviour of the headmaster and his Ngoni wife, listened to some of the lessons in school, watched the boys 'drill' in the playground, he ordered all Ngoni boys and girls in the village to attend school, and arranged a roster for cattle-herding, so that the boys would learn herding as well as their school lessons. He sent for the headmaster to report to him periodically on how the children were behaving, and which ones were showing particular aptitudes. The young headmaster showed characteristic Ngoni ability to organize his school, control his staff, demand and get good behaviour from the children. He was, like the evangelist, a huntsman of repute, and he was too a good dancer, and had a judgement in public affairs that was acknowledged to be beyond his years.

The aversion shown in the other Ngoni village described in Chapter I to schools and to missions generally arose partly from the fact that there were no Ngoni teachers or ministers serving that area. The teachers in near-by schools were from a tribe whom the Ngoni despised and whose personal habits they deplored. The missions in the area had made no attempt to integrate schoolteaching and preaching in the churches with Ngoni life and thought. Some Ngoni fathers sent their boys to the Scottish Mission boarding-school in Blantyre, and were willing to pay the fees because they knew and believed in those in charge of that school.

Ngoni fathers, and this was true of both areas, expected their boys who had been to school and had entered European employment away from their homes, to find work which assured them a superior and not an inferior or unskilled position. They wanted them to be, or to become, senior clerks, trusted store assistants, valued houseboys, foremen in charge of other men, hospital assistants. They wanted them, in other words, to be in positions where Ngoni traits would be appreciated, and where good behaviour and self-control, ability to supervise others, responsibility and initiative, obedience to orders, would be recognized and rewarded.

In conclusion here is a record of a conversation I heard in the village of a very senior chief, so senior that he was given the title of *Inkosi* when his subjects addressed him. The chief, who was then in his seventies, but active and vigorous, was sitting in a chair on the veranda of his hut, out of the sun's glare, with several of the senior men of the village behind him. Two young teachers in charge of a school came to greet him. They bent one knee as they squatted in front of him, as they had been taught to do as children, gave him the customary greeting, and waited in silence till he spoke.

'How is your school?'

'The classes are full and the children are learning well, *Inkosi.*'

'How do they behave?'

'Like Ngoni children, *Inkosi.*'

'What do they learn?'

'They learn reading, writing and arithmetic, scripture and geography and drill.'

'Is that education?'

'It is education, *Inkosi.*'

'No! No! Education is *very* broad, *very* deep. It is not only in books, it is learning to live. I am an old man. When I was a boy I went with the army to the Bemba war. Then the mission came and I went to school. I became a teacher. Then I was a chief. I have seen this country change, and now the young men go away to work. I tell you Ngoni children must learn how to live, and how to work and earn money, and how to build up our land. *Uyezwa na?*' (Do you hear?)

'*Yebo Inkosi.*' (Yes, O chief.)

IX

Some Educational Reflections

Education, culture and society

We saw in the introduction that the main objective in this study was to see what the Ngoni parents were aiming at in bringing up their children, and how they had worked out a system which they believed suitable for their society. It was suggested that some of the aims and methods used by the Ngoni might throw light on some of the problems which faced young parents and teachers today. This does not mean of course that the methods used by the Ngoni are in any sense transferable to other peoples and other times. They were tried out in and related to a specific situation. Nor does it mean that the aims of the Ngoni in their education could be in any way compared with parental aims in bringing up children in our own day and age, and in our own society. The very sharp contrast between Ngoni life and thought, and our own ideas and our present situation, makes any kind of close comparison invalid and a waste of time. What we have to try to do, if this study has stimulated us to think more deeply about these matters, is to understand the relation between aims and methods in the Ngoni system of education, and to stretch our own concept of education beyond the limits of formal learning and regular schooling to include what many American educationists call 'adjustment to life'.

American educational thinking is turning more and more towards social and cultural anthropology as a guide to analysing educational problems in their schools, in their homes, in their communities and in their national life. There are several reasons for this tendency. One is a recognition of the limitations of individual psychology as a guide to the understanding of how children grow up. This arises from the newly perceived importance of culture, in the anthropological sense of that word, as a total way of living of a specific group of people, which may be that of a fairly homogeneous large group, or of several smaller groups, differing culturally from each other but drawn together by political, economic or residential ties. Thus Ngoni culture as described in this book could be regarded as that of a small group within the Ngoni kingdom and within Ngoni villages where other people of differing cultures were to be found. A number of references were made in this study to the cultural differences within Ngoni villages in spite of the proximity of living conditions. We find the same kind of situation in many countries today, whether those of a western way of living or a non-western. The French Swiss in Switzerland for example are a distinct cultural group within the Swiss nation, and they are divided into the sub-cultural groups of Protestants and Catholics, each with a characteristic way of living which shows itself not only in differences of religious belief.

As we look round the world we see societies, even nations or parts of nations like the French Swiss, trying to hold on either to their total culture, or to those parts of it such as language, religion, forms of family life, distinctive dress and food, which seem to them to have special significance for them and their children. No cultures, or virtually none, are unaffected by modern changes brought about by political, economic or social influences and forces. And there are societies and nations anxious to change their culture in order to bring it into line with the demands of modern, mainly western, life. The educationist who is aware of other systems than his own soon realizes that an education system and what is taught in it can be used to change culture, or to perpetuate certain elements in it. This attempt to balance the forces of cultural change and cultural continuity through the education of a people is found all over the world today.

The concept of culture as a way of living, and of a specific society or social group practising that way of living, has many implications for those who are thinking about education at the present time. Readers of this book, especially those in western countries, who are unaccustomed to the ideas and language of anthropology, may find some difficulty in relating what they have thought of as principles of education to the aims and methods of the Ngoni in bringing up their children. This difficulty arises for two main reasons. One is that we in the west have to stretch and widen our ideas about education, and burst the classroom walls in our effort to see children growing up in a total culture and not only inside the limits of formal schooling. The other reason also demands an effort of imagination, for we in the west have got to appreciate and understand the differences between the growing up of children in the tight little family of father, mother and children living a separate existence in a town house or flat, and children growing up in the larger family and circle of relatives, creating family life in the wider sense used in this Ngoni study. The first kind of family life is characteristic of our urban industrial society, the second of rural life in most of the rest of the world and in many aspects of urban life in eastern and African countries as well.

The inevitable sequel, or at least it should always follow, to thinking about education as either changing a people's culture or helping to perpetuate parts of it, is to look at the effect on individual children and their growth and development. This concentration on individual development has so far been the main preoccupation of educational study in the west, and many questions arise, as was suggested in the introduction, about the effect, for example, of certain Ngoni methods of training on the development of individuals. Perhaps all students of education, and most administrators and planners too, have to ride a see-saw between adapting education to the needs of society and adapting it to the needs of individual children. There is as we all know no final choice possible. Some kind of synthesis is essential, and the balance is always swinging first in one direction and then in another. And here parents, their views on education and their methods of training children in their homes, have a supremely important role to play, almost a controlling role, since they can work in with the aims of formal schooling or persistently try to counteract them.

Where this study might lead

'Growing up among the Ngoni' is only one of several studies of growing up in non-western societies. The societies described from this angle of child-training differ from each other structurally and culturally, but there are common elements in the studies of growing up which should be of interest, in western and non-western countries alike, to teachers and parents and all who are concerned about how children are in fact growing up, and the role of formal schooling in this process.

One of the dominant notes in modern psychological advice to young parents and to teachers is the emphasis on security for the young child. It is worth while looking at the early years of Ngoni children from this angle, and perhaps using other studies of growing up as well, examining the kind of security provided by a wide circle of relatives all living round the child's home, and all ready to meet the child's needs; and then comparing this form of security with the dependence of a young child on its mother only, which is characteristic of most small families in western urban societies.

There is another aspect of the security of Ngoni children, found too in several other growing up studies, and that is the freedom conferred on a child because he learns early in life just how to speak and how to behave to other people. This may be an unusual view of the apparent restrictions placed on language, posture, attitude, actions, displayed by a child particularly towards adults. Anyone who has brought up children however knows that they are unhappy with unlimited licence in behaviour, and is aware that the learning of etiquette and manners and obedience, apparently so tiresome in its early stages, does eventually eliminate a number of perplexing choices for children, and by regulating certain relationships confers freedom in other directions. That was my reading of the Ngoni children's reactions to the somewhat formal code of manners taught from their early years and strictly enforced. Ngoni good manners did not mean that the children were coerced and subdued. They were happy, busy, friendly, helpful, endlessly inventive and full of initiative. I suggested here and there in the book that they had various outlets in the middle years of childhood for aggression, jealousy, frustration. There was very little evidence of neurotic tendencies, and, except in certain instances mentioned, there was little apparent inclination to avoid social mixing with age-mates or with other groups and the obligations inherent in such mixing.

The seeming absence of frustration and overt rebellion in the years just after puberty was due to the social recognition by relatives and by the village community of the new stage reached by boys and girls, and to the increasing responsibility required of them for carrying out allotted tasks and for preparing for their future careers. There was no doubt that the outlet for youths of emigration from the villages to work for wages in the south provided a much-needed opportunity at a critical moment in their late teens. In the same way the stimulus of modern schooling, depending on the area and the type of schools in it, helped older boys and girls to look forward to further opportunities of work, of interests, and of escape from the too intimate control of their family and kinship circle and village elders.

Another line to be followed in these growing-up studies is the actual pattern of relationships between the parents and the children, the parents and their circle of relatives, the parents and the community, the children and the community, and the community and the school. There are a number of clues to follow in examining the different groups of people involved in a child's growing up, and discovering some kind of consistent pattern of relationship between them. The clues are not difficult to trace for they begin in such information as the amount of time a child spends with each group, what he learns from each group, how much authority and responsibility the group assumes for him, and so on. In this analysis it is not enough to relate each group to the children. It is important too to be aware of the personal relations between parents, relatives, community, school authorities, in terms of their opportunities for mutual contact and discussion, and their attitude towards culture change and cultural conservation. Out of such potential contacts arise the formulation of aims for home and school training, and their harmony or their conflict, and the resultant effects on the growing up of a child.

These two lines to be followed up, which we have just indicated, are familiar to most teachers and to many parents. The third line arising out of this study, and common to most other studies of growing up, is related to research on personality and culture and on national character. This field of studies is more controversial and more complex than the former. In the case of the Ngoni they had a more or less distinct ideal personality rooted in their culture and answering the question: what kind of people are the Ngoni and how do they want others to regard them? This ideal personality was the goal of their child-training as described in this book, but it was in the process of being modified by school teaching, by Christian teaching, and perhaps more profoundly still by the growth of Nyasaland African nationalism. The sharp outlines of the ideal personality type of Ngoni men and women were already blurred by these political and educational developments.

For readers of this book the relevance of this aspect of

Ngoni children's growing up is probably to call attention to cultural and national influences in emphasizing certain qualities in the ideal personality and in individual character.

In general, in the west, cultural influences determining a way of life, and setting standards for individual behaviour are found in certain kinds of 'class' grouping, or in the environmental determinants of rural communities, 'new' towns and housing estates, slum or suburban areas. Very few western societies can show their children the sharp outline of an ideal personality which seemed so important and compelling to the Ngoni. Nevertheless behind parents' attempts to train their children or to direct their growing up lie as a rule some vague ideas about ideal personality traits or the qualities to be looked for in national character. Perhaps some searching into these fundamental motives, stimulated by this Ngoni study, could help to bring them to the surface and so assist in the harmonizing of educational aims.

Appendix

I

SELECT BIBLIOGRAPHY

AMMAR, H. M., *Growing up in an Egyptian village*. Kegan Paul 1954. The introduction has a survey of relevant literature in this field.

CIBAMBO, Y. M., *My Ngoni of Nyasaland*. Lutterworth Press, 1942. Ngoni history and culture by a leading Ngoni minister.

ELLIOT, GERALDINE, *The Long Grass Whispers*. Routledge, 1939. A collection of folk tales from Ngoniland.

FIRTH R., 1. *Elements of Social Organisation*. Watts & Co. 1951. A technical description of social anthropology.
2. *Human Types*. Nelson Revised edition 1956. Introduction to social anthropology.

FORTES, M., *Social and Psychological Aspects of Education in Taleland*. International African Institute Memorandum No. 17—1938. A pioneer study in the Northern Territories of Ghana.

KLUCKHOHN C., *Mirror for man: the relation of anthropology to modern life*. McGraw Hill, 1948. A particularly useful section on Personality and Culture.

LEIGHTON, D. AND KLUCKHOHN, C., *Children of the People*. Harvard University Press, 1949. Growing up among the Navaho Indians of New Mexico, U.S.A.

LEWIS, OSCAR, *Life in a Mexican village*. University of Illinois Press 1951. Useful section on relation of school and community.

LINTON R., *The cultural background of personality*. Kegan Paul, 1947. The most useful analysis of these problems.

MEAD, MARGARET, 1. *Coming of age in Samoa*. Cape, 1929. Penguins, 1943.

2. *Growing up in New Guinea*. Kegan Paul, 1939—Penguin, 1954. These were two pioneer studies in the Pacific.

3. *New Worlds for Old*. Gollancz, 1956. The New Guinea area was revisited after 25 years. See especially chapters V, XIII and XIV for Dr. Mead's assessment of her former study.

RAUM, OTTO, *Chaga Childhood*, Oxford University Press, 1940. A pioneer study of child training in Tanganyika. His introductory survey of literature has been superseded by that of H. M. Ammar.

READ, MARGARET, 1. *The Ngoni of Nyasaland*. Oxford University Press, 1956. A full scale study of Ngoni culture and social organization.

2. *Education and Social Change in Tropical Areas*. Nelson, 1955. See especially the papers on Anthropology and Education (page 68), and Cultural Contacts in Education (page 96).

3. *Education and Cultural Tradition*. Evans, 1950. Inaugural lecture on the study of child training in non-literate societies.

RICHARDS, AUDREY, 1. *Chisungu*. Faber, 1956. A study of girls' initiation rites in Northern Rhodesia.

WHITING, J. W. K., 1. *Becoming a Kwoma*. Yale University Press, 1941. A pioneer study in the Pacific.

2. *Field Manual on Child Training Studies*. Havard, 1955. A valuable guide to field workers in non-literate societies.

WILSON, MONICA, *Good Company*. Oxford University Press, 1951· A study of the Nyakusa age-village in Tanganyika.

II

DEFINITIONS

CULTURE, the total way of living of a people, including kinship relations, economy, religion and magic, law, government, language, myths, child training etc.

ETHNIC GROUP, used here instead of tribe because the Ngoni kingdoms and villages included several tribes. (See Ngoni of Nyasaland p. 1–6).

CLAN, exogamous group related through male line with a common clan name used in address. True Ngoni clans formed the aristocracy (See Ngoni of Nyasaland p. 116).

HOUSE, HUT, HOUSEHOLD, house is used in this book for the Ngoni system of grouping round the leading women who were wives or mothers of the head of the village. Hut is used for the actual building. Household is used for a group of huts within a compound, (See diagrams in Chapter IV. See also Ngoni of Nyasaland page 122).

PATRILOCAL), refers to residence of young couple after marriage

MATRILOCAL), —sometimes called virilocal and uxorilocal.

CLASSIFICATORY KINSHIP TERMS, extension of use of father, mother, brother, sister etc. to wide range of relatives.

PARALLEL COUSINS, children of father's brothers or mother's sisters—regarded as brothers and sisters and called such.

CROSS COUSINS, children of father's sisters or mother's brothers— with whom marriage was possible.

AGE-SETS, the special Ngoni terms are given in 'Ngoni of Nyasaland' page 144.

all children: *abantwana*

young men: *amajaha*

young girls before puberty: *inkakazana*

young girls after puberty: *izintombi*

III
VERNACULAR TERMS

AKULU	the important people
ALEZI	nursemaids
GOGO	grandparent or any very senior person
HLONIPA	respect
INDLUNKULU	chief hut in a village
INDUNA	official in village
IZIDANDANI	girl attendants
LAWENI	boys' dormitory
MWINI	owner—of a hut, cattle, dance group

NDUKU	knobkerry—club with rounded end.
NGOMA	Ngoni dance for older boys and girls
NTONGA	a rod or long pole
NYANJA	most common vernacular in Nyasaland
SANGWENI	gate of cattle kraal
ULEMU	respect
UMSINDO	pre-marriage rite for girls